BARTS AND T
SCHOOL OF MEDICIN
WHITECHAPEL

SOMATIC ILLNESS AND THE PATIENT'S *OTHER* STORY

SOMATIC ILLNESS AND THE PATIENT'S *OTHER* STORY

A Practical Integrative Mind/Body
Approach to Disease for
Doctors and Psychotherapists

BRIAN BROOM

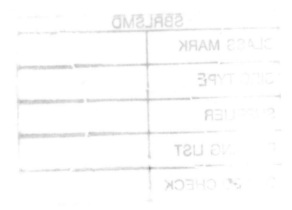

FREE ASSOCIATION BOOKS / LONDON / NEW YORK

Published in 1997 by
Free Association Books Ltd
57 Warren Street, London W1P 5PA
and 70 Washington Square South,
New York, NY 10012–1091

ISBN 1 85343 379 9 hardback

A CIP catalogue record for this book is available from
the British Library.

Produced for Free Association Books by
Chase Production Services, Chadlington, OX7 3LN
Printed and bound by Antony Rowe Ltd, Eastbourne

Contents

TO ALISON

PREFACE AND ACKNOWLEDGEMENTS

I have a passion for integrative approaches to healing. I get impatient with the artificial boundaries which neatly carve up health care in ways which, whilst maintaining professional identity and quality control, bring implicit constriction of paradigmatic vision and therapeutic modality. I cannot entirely explain this passion though I am sure early life influences have played some part (just as they have for the many patients and clients mentioned in this book). I grew up in a semi-rural setting where we made our own entertainment, and adventure, and explored far and wide, neither constrained by nor blessed with the many laid-on orthodox opportunities and ultimately conforming structures of a middle-class upbringing. I think the overall impact of this was an implicit environmental invitation to range and roam. I didn't really discover until high school that, in contrast, most of my peers were acculturated to very high performance within very well defined and strictly socially acceptable bounds. Though I have since at times lamented my lack of preparation for that 'real' world, I am increasingly grateful for my early experience of an environment without rigid bounds.

But, inevitably, this is just part of the story. Despite the freedoms described above there were in fact other contrasting constraints and pressures to conform, arising from my family's involvement in Christian faith. These constraints were sufficiently subcultural to engender early experience of social margination, something which has had its difficulties, but also unexpected benefits in that it probably contributed to a certain willingness to risk and tolerate (but certainly not enjoy) professional isolation and collegial scepticism, things which have been part of my experience in the journey of exploration of the 'margins'. I use the word 'margins' because those pursuing mind/body/spirit integrative endeavours still remain at the edge of orthodox practice in the current physico-materialist medical climate. I regard myself as an orthodox practitioner endeavouring to integrate in crucial elements excluded by the current constrictive paradigm.

But the climate is changing. I have experienced considerable welcome for the propositions in this book from both family doctors and psychotherapists, and there have been many requests for a written presentation. I have considered specialist doctors more wary and sceptical, but I am now not so sure about this. For example, recently I presented the essentials of my approach (in a talk entitled 'Allergy and Story: Mixing Medicine and Psychotherapy') to peer Australasian clinical immunologists and allergists, and I was both surprised and gratified by the interest and openness. Certainly some want more evidence based on measurement data, but I now realise that even hard-core scientists find it hard not to resonate intuitively with the relevance of personal 'story' in illness and disease. Such resonance is sometimes only transient because the implications are too disturbing or threatening.

There are other still obscure roots to this integrative passion. I chose a career in medicine at the age of ten. I remember making the announcement to my mother whilst washing rather grubby legs after a day in the paddocks. Maybe it had something to do with the occasional visit to the family doctor for undiagnosed abdominal pain, presumably somatisation. There was certainly no family precedent for higher education. I trained in medicine at the University of Otago Medical School, and soon discovered the powerful (and often shaming) forces at work which conspire to produce very safe orthodox clinicians who have very little capacity or desire to look beyond the dominant dualistic physico-materialist paradigm of disease and healing. I performed reasonably well in this ethos, specialised in internal medicine (in the field of clinical immunology and allergy), and under the generous auspices of a New Zealand Medical Research Council Training Fellowship obtained research and clinical training in Birmingham, London and Montreal. I returned to New Zealand as a medical school teacher and researcher, and set up a clinical immunology department. But, increasingly, I felt locked into a highly scientific physicalist focus, and eventually moved into psychiatry to broaden my clinical capabilities. Psychiatry training was a stimulating experience, but I found the discipline just as dualistic as internal medicine, and whilst respecting the need for psychiatry to explore the clinical potential of biological aspects of mental functioning, I had, not unexpectedly, little patience with the increasingly dominant biological ideology gripping psychiatry. I was more interested in psychotherapy for its emphasis on the nonphysical aspects of personal functioning, and eventually decided to blend psychotherapy practice with clinical immunology practice, the latter enabling me to keep in focus the physical aspects of personal functioning. In this way I set up the clinical context in which to explore the integration of mind and body aspects of illness and disease. I say more about this in Chapter 2.

Hovering around this interest in mind/body integration is an interest in spirit. I work at the Arahura (New Zealand indigenous peoples' term for 'pathway to discovery') Christian Counselling and Medical Centre, a centre I set up in 1986 with two others to enable professional practice in a setting where the exploration of integrative aspects of healing is facilitated. I am enormously grateful to my colleagues at Arahura: to Murray Winn and John Smalley for joining with me originally to develop the initial critical mass for the venture; to Graeme Wright for his unfailing friendship and support; to Murray Winn, Ainslie McDowall, Derek Willis, Graeme Wright and Jan Young for their willingness to work alongside me with somatising clientele; and to all the professional and ancillary staff and trainees who contribute to the rare institutional intimacy and supportiveness we enjoy at Arahura. It is certainly a place where I have felt both freedom to explore my individual potential, and to enjoy the communal solidarity which has been so important in the hard times. It is also a place where there is a commitment to professional rigour and competence, and to the development of people, including aspects of spirit; a place where spirit is not defined too narrowly. I hope that eventually I will be able to offer written commentary on aspects of spirit in disease and healing, which will be supplementary to the mind/body aspects offered in this book. I touch on these issues in Chapter 10, but this side has to grow more.

I am very grateful to the patients with physical symptoms who have trusted me enough to enter psychotherapy, and with whom I have discovered a breathtaking panorama of mind/body connections, and who recovered health often enough to embolden me to stretch my boundaries and presuppositions further and further. It is impossible to write a book like this without telling patients' stories. I have gone to great length to remove or alter details which might identify patients and clients. Any likeness to known individuals may be attributed to the commonness of certain conditions, the 'universality' of many human dilemmas, and, finally, coincidence. In addition, in the first case in Chapter 1, and in the long cases in Chapters 2 and 7, I have asked these individuals to read the material and give consent. I am extremely grateful to these three generous people. Additional thanks go to Michael Harlow, friend and psychotherapist colleague, who (as well as working with a lot of my referrals) kept this neophyte author on track towards a pub-

lisher; to Gill Davies, at Free Association Books, whose real interest in the work, engaging communications, and sense of humour
greatly enlivened the final publishing process; and to Robert Craw-
ford, psychiatrist and psychotherapist, friend and peer-supervisor,
who has supported me through the real and imagined practical
difficulties of communicating my point of view to the medical
profession.

Finally, and most importantly, my family: I am deeply indebted
to my wife, Alison, who has been unremittingly generous, supportive, optimistic and believing of the value of the work. More than
that – when I have been transiently lost in the complexity of the
journey, her direct, intelligent instinct for what is true and really
important has been repeatedly helpful. My children Sarah, Jennifer
and Alex have not only been interested and supportive, but good-
humouredly tolerant of my dinner-table talk around mind/body/
spirit issues, whilst not infrequently bringing me down to earth by
pointing out other points of view and possibilities.

1 SEEING OR NOT SEEING

He may be called wild because of his passionate nature which wants to help where others have resigned or are hiding their impotence behind the mock techniques of exact diagnostics ... Groddeck's wildness is also the hatred with which he fights the old-fashioned medical practices by which, before Freud, the doctor was placed in the centre of the healing situation instead of the patient, out of a kind of medical narcissism ... He uniquely fits the distinction made by the philosopher Georg Simmel between artist and scientist: 'The scientist sees because he knows, the artist knows because he sees.' We know or seek to know what we can get by learning. Groddeck sees and knows without making this detour. (Schact 1977, pp. 7–8)

It's about seeing or not seeing. The modern doctor is rigorously educated, but the education is received from experts, from those who always know more than the student, and certainly more than the patient. Much of this education is of great value, but the pivot around expertise means that students learn to operate out of deference to received knowledge; they end up seeing only that which they have learned. There are some things which cannot be learned, and one of these is the *meaning* of a patient's illness. This must be discovered by the patient and clinician working collaboratively.

The Story

This book is about putting the patient's unique story, along with the doctor's received learning, at the centre of the healing enterprise. The patient's story is, amongst many other things, a woven tapestry – of events, of perceptions of events, and of highly idiosyncratic responses to events. Many of the very significant events have to do with the vicissitudes of the patient's relationships with the world, and with other significant persons. Therefore, when a patient and a doctor collaborate together to look for the meaning of an illness, they are usually looking for the story of a person in relationship.

Inevitably there are other layers of complexity. The doctor him-self[1] also has a unique story, and that story powerfully conditions how the doctor will (or can) respond to the patient. Furthermore the patient and the doctor are in a highly complex relationship conditioned by their respective stories. This book says as much about how clinicians might think and behave within the therapeutic relationship as it does about the meaning of illness based on an understanding of the patient's individual story.

To complicate things further an integrative mind/body approach to the healing enterprise must include the elements highly honoured by modern medicine: the patient brings to the encounter his disease, and the doctor brings his learned scientific expertise. Too often these are the only elements honoured in the medical enterprise. Nevertheless it would be foolish, in reaction to this taxonomic and scientific reductionism, to commit the opposite sin of reducing all illness to *story*. The following case is a remarkable example of the relationship between 'powerful story' and 'serious diagnosis'. Disregard of either has serious implications.

T. requested review because she wanted to 'live life more fully'. In her thirties she developed leukoplakia, a precancerous condition of the mouth. By the time she came to me she had had seven surgical interventions, including removal of carcinoma and plastic reconstructions of the tongue and the floor of the mouth – the last requiring eighteen months' rehabilitation as she learned to speak again. Early in the interview she proffered the interesting comment that, 'If only I could get rid of it [my emphasis] I would be able to live more fully from day to day.' Though she was obviously (!) referring to the leukoplakia and cancerous tendency, I suspected the it was not the cancer which had been removed two years before, with no evidence of recurrence. I noted the words but made no comment.

A review of her life story was illuminating, and some key points will be emphasised. Apparently, after she was born, she and her mother were collected by father from the hospital. He dropped them off at home and went off to see his mistress. When T. was seven years old her father committed suicide, though she was not aware of the nature of his death. At age twelve she was crying in her bedroom. Mother found her, asked what was wrong, and T. replied she was

---

[1] In an attempt to avoid clumsiness and gender preference I will use male or female in any one chapter.

crying about 'Daddy'. Mother, who was by then an alcoholic, responded: 'It's your fault your father is dead – you would never sit on his knee.' The background to this cruel comment is not entirely clear. T. did remember that as a child she often felt she identified much more with her absent father than with her mother. At age sixteen she learned from relatives that her father had committed suicide. At nineteen she entered a marriage that, over six years, repeated in some ways the traumas of childhood. At age thirty-three she developed leukoplakia of the mouth. I learned that this was the age that her father had committed suicide. Her father was an oral surgeon. I pointed this out to T. who had herself wondered, over the years, whether this was significant, though it had never been discussed with doctors. Returning in my mind to the it referred to above, I asked her what, apart from this cancerous tendency, she would most like to get rid of in her life. She seemed to understand what I was asking, but struggled initially, becoming very tearful, unable to find the right word. Eventually she said she most wanted to get rid of the shame. To me it seemed likely that the shame and the leukoplakia were intimately connected in some way. Could one think up a better somatic metaphor than a precancerous condition of the mouth, for the shame of being responsible for the death of one's oral surgeon father?

If this woman's story were known, and taken seriously, when she was thirty-three, and if the shame had been resolved, would she have run the same clinical course? Would this cancerous tendency remit if she underwent psychotherapy? In fact she did have some brief psychotherapy, which was unusually fast-moving and involved only nine sessions. A year later she reported no further problems and her surgeon expressed some astonishment with the good state of her mouth. It is difficult to be sure of the significance of these observations. Perhaps more compelling is the fact that the turning point in therapy occurred when she actually started to remember sitting on her father's knee. She reported, after the session in which that occurred, a persistent 'joy' which has continued, and seems to have expressed itself in a variety of interpersonal and social freedoms. She also reports now that for the first time in her life she finds herself considering living into her eighties. Only time will confirm these apparent indications of positive psychotherapeutic impact upon the leukoplakia.

This book is about what can happen when one takes seriously these putative connections between the presenting physical symptoms and the patient's story. Many clinical examples will be given of the relevance of these connections to the healing of the patient, but the main intention is to assist the doctor and the psychotherapist to work well with patients and clients by using a clinically practical mind/body approach.

The particular clinical group of concern here is comprised of people who, in the first place, come to the clinician (usually the medical doctor) with physical symptoms. The clinician is willing to listen for the 'story', and this story is taken as very important and relevant, in some way, to the physical illness presentation. The clinician encourages the patient to undergo an exploration of the connections between symptoms and story and, in many cases, the result is restoration to health, or at least a loss of the physical symptoms.

Somatiser and Somatisation

The focus is on the person as a whole. This person presents to the clinician with symptoms in the body. The bodily symptoms are considered carefully, along with the 'story' of the whole person, and a working hypothesis is developed as to the meaning of the symptoms. The clinician and patient then join in a collaborative journey of discovery and healing.

In the mind/body area terminology is fraught with difficulties. In this book the term 'somatiser' refers to persons who are somatic symptom *presenters*, and the term 'somatisation' refers to persons with somatic symptom *presentations*. It is acknowledged that this usage is not highly specific.

In utilising terms such as somatiser and somatisation there is acknowledgement here of their common usage in psychiatry. There is a paucity of suitable alternatives, and it does not seem appropriate at this point to try and create new terms, but rather to push to use them somewhat differently. Later in this chapter there will be further discussion of nomenclature including other psychiatric terms used in the mind/body disorder territory, such as 'somatisation disorder' or 'somatoform disorder'.

But it should be clearly understood how somatiser and somatisation are being used here. One emphasises the person as present*er* of physical symptoms and the other emphasises the present*ation* of physical symptoms. Psychiatric readers in particular need to realise that the terms are not being used in the more dualistic way they will be accustomed to.

Moreover, the emphasis is also upon viewing the presenting physical symptom as the superficial expression of something deeper and wider, or, alternatively stated, as one aspect of the multifaceted unitary reality, which is commonly called 'person' (this will be clarified in detail in Chapter 9). The person is thus seen as presenting his self (which emerges in the context of the influences of both nature and nurture), in the 'language' of the body. In this sense he is a somatiser, and the physical manifestation is a somatisation. It is important to say at this point that although symptom-as-language is an important concept it must not be carried too far (see Chapter 10).

Though others might construe somatisation rather more narrowly, as a conversion of emotional reality into bodily terms or idiom, the use here is wider, and allows for other possibilities such as viewing the physical symptom or disease as the somatic face of the story of the whole which has other dimensions such as the psychological, spiritual and social. The justification for this approach will become clearer as we proceed.

The Problem of Case Selection

The clinical experience offered in this book has accumulated in work with *selected* patients.[2] First, many fall into the categories of clinical presentation found in an allergy referral practice.

[2] Since 1987 our energies have been devoted to establishing clinically effective methods of working with individual somatisers, as well as developing a team of psychotherapists with the required skills. During 1993, 300 new referrals were assessed in the allergy and clinical immunology practice. All were assessed (in the first interview) from both a somatic and a psychological point of view. At times the psychological assessment was left at a superficial level, especially when it appeared that the presenting complaint could be adequately and pragmatically dealt with using conventional orthodox medical treatments. Eventually there were 124 out of the 300 who, assessed from both somatic and psychological vantage points, were judged to be, and treated as, somatisers with significant collateral 'stories' or psychological aspects, and who were recommended through to psychotherapy. Though all 124 were offered psychotherapy only 58 finally engaged in therapy (reasons for failure to engage are given in the main text). All of this latter group were eventually sent a questionnaire which included enquiry regarding symptom levels both at the end of therapy and at the time of the survey, which for most patients was many months after the end of therapy. Twenty-six returned their questionnaires, and it is from this group that most of the short clinical histories detailed have been selected, using case histories which were sufficiently common in type, or able to be altered in such a way as to preserve confidentiality.

In New Zealand there is a common belief that allergy practice attracts 'neurotic' patients. It is unlikely that allergy practice attracts more mind/body disorders than other types of medical practice, but it does attract a group of somatisers who tend to externalise their problems, and misattribute them to exogenous factors such as foods, for example. It is assumed here that in other types of medical practice mind/body disorders are frequent, but it may be that the underlying 'forces' leading to the particular illness presentation may be rather different to those leading to allergy. It is possible that somatisers in non-allergy settings would be less inclined by personality structure to an externalising or projective defensive explanation for their symptomatology (the need to find an external causative agent such as food might be construed as a manifestation of a projective defensive style).

Second, the patients described are selected in the sense that the recommendation to psychotherapy is based on the author's *current* pattern of deciding who will be regarded as a somatiser and who will not. It could be that all patients presenting with physical symptoms are somatisers (a conceptual position which rigorously rejects both dualism and physicalism might assert this), or that patients who are not offered psychotherapy are in fact somatisers and are missing out.

For example, a patient presented with severe allergy to grass pollen and deer dander allergens. This could be handled satisfactorily in an orthodox way with a pure biological approach. Testing showed clear immunological evidence of allergy to the deer and grass allergens and she was offered treatment by immunotherapy. Therefore a very somatic approach to the problem was adopted. But in talking to the patient it was clear that there was a very deep ambivalence to her role in the family's deer farm, and it appeared that the psychological need to maintain family stability was greater than the need to work out the underlying hostilities. It can be speculated that the deer allergy was not only a manifestation of deer contact, but also a metaphor for, and a partial symbolic working out of, these hostilities. Nevertheless, a psychotherapy approach was not suggested, the main reasons being the patient's remote geographical location, her lack of psychological-mindedness, the lack of available local psychotherapy expertise, and lack of clinical conviction (and a lack of evidence) that the deer allergy was due to this hypothesis or could be treated by psychotherapy. Finally, there was a readily available conventional therapy.

The author had some misgivings about this pragmatic approach mainly because this patient's clinical history was littered with other somatic disorders which were almost certainly manifestations of emotional turmoil. If the allergies were successfully treated using purely somatic approaches, and the deer allergy was in fact a somatisation of underlying psychological issues, it was conceivable that the patient would at some stage present with some other somatic expression of the underlying unresolved themes and conflicts. In this case the chosen somatic approach was immediately helpful, it was pragmatic and practical, and nonidealistic. But if she went on to get other disorders because she was not being helped to face the real underlying issues, it was also in part collusive. In the end the clinical approach had defined her as a biological problem rather than a somatiser and this may be incorrect. She had been selected this way for pragmatic reasons.

Sometimes the pragmatic approach proves very unsatisfactory, and it is only too apparent that the application of a highly effective biological therapy is just not enough. A patient may be selected for a biological treatment and regarded as a nonsomatiser, but in the end one wonders whether that really has been the right decision. For example, another patient developed a severe allergy to bee stings whilst assisting his father in their jointly owned apiary. Desensitisation, by injection, with bee venom is the orthodox and highly effective approach to this dangerous allergy, and this was commenced. But early on his deep ambivalence to his role in the family business, and its adverse psychosocial implications for him, was clearly recognisable to staff, though he was unable to acknowledge this. During the desensitisation process there was great difficulty with very unusual side-effects to the treatment, but eventually a dosage was achieved which would normally be highly effective. It was only when he got to the point where the symptoms and side-effects could no longer be attributed either to the allergy or to the therapy, that he began to acknowledge his 'allergy' to his wider situation. It was only as he started to work through the emotional aspects that the severe side-effects started to settle. The pragmatic biological approach was not sufficient in this case.

These clinical examples are probably the tip of the iceberg and, if so, there may be many somatisers who are not offered useful psychotherapy. Most clinicians are constrained by their current understanding, and also by ethical propositions which assert that to offer such therapy to patients when there are orthodox therapies available, which provide satisfactory if not perfect assistance and relief, is probably unwise until there is established a sound and well researched basis for a different approach.

Third, the patients who have undergone psychotherapy are selected in the sense that these are the ones who eventually accepted the offer of psychotherapy. In terms of potential response to psychotherapy they may be a very different group to those who did not finally engage in therapy. A number of the latter group failed to engage because they had to wait too long for a therapist, lost heart, and 'fell off' the waiting list. The engagement success rate is much better when there are minimal waiting times between initial assessment and the commencement of therapy. Others appear to get better with just the responses, interventions and explanations provided in the initial allergy work-up process.

Finally, many of the illustrative and introductory clinical examples presented here are self-selected because they are individuals who chose to respond to a questionnaire. There are many reasons why patients fail to complete a questionnaire, and these constitute a selective element.

Twelve Examples of Physical Disorders Treated with a Mind/ Body Approach

The therapist involved in each case will be designated A, B, C, and so on. Commentary will be provided on some cases so as not to lose their unique instructive potential, because they are not presented again later in the book.

Case 1

A man aged thirty-five presented with a two-year history of lethargy, dizziness, forehead rash, abdominal bloating, diarrhoea, constipation, night sweats, air hunger, myalgias, arthralgias, back and neck pain, nocturnal urinary frequency, haematuria (of unknown cause, and resolved when assessed by me), sneezing, poor concentration, restless sleep and early morning wakening. He had previously been a fit man who 'collapsed' whilst running, after a period of prolonged work stress. He felt as if he was finally 'caving in'. He was willing to try psychotherapy with therapist D, but expressed mild scepticism. A major theme was a need to perform 'at the top', and a view of the self as 'indestructible'. He was a man who 'never gave up' but in the end was forced to (and finally 'caved in'), with ensuing guilt, and loss of worth. He had a total of eighteen sessions and achieved 90 per cent improvement in symptoms, though he was left with some residual sleep disturbance.

The 'caving in' metaphor evident here is of great interest. In many somatisers symptoms occur in almost every system. In some cases it seems to reflect the feeling that the 'whole of me' is weak or cannot cope. In psychodynamic terms it often reflects 'all or nothing' thinking. Any acknowledgement of weakness may be seen as a collapse of the whole. As psychotherapist readers will know, this theme comes in many variations.

Case 2

A woman aged twenty-nine presented with three years of fatigue, fluctuating cervical lymphadenopathy, frequent upper respiratory tract infections and sore throat, muscle spasm headaches, aching neck, urinary frequency, nausea, flatus, abdominal bloating, aching feet, limb paraesthesia, irritability and social anxiety. There was great difficulty in talking about feelings, and she tended to 'control' sessions. She allowed some access to feelings of loneliness, unimportance, badness, powerlessness and sadness. She started to read books on feelings and reported increased communication with friends. Collaterally certain aspects of her social and work situation became less stressful. She reported a large reduction in symptoms though she stayed in formal psychotherapy for only three sessions. Therapist D remained guarded as to her prognosis.

Some patients will improve quite rapidly and this can occur after initial assessment even before psychotherapy starts. There seems to be a variety of reasons for this. Mere reassurance that they are not suffering from sinister illnesses may be enough. Some seem to get well when they get the right diagnosis. For instance even knowing that the problem is psychologically based may be enough. This is testimony to the illness-perpetuating effects of a false somatic paradigm for that illness. Other patients do well with a minimal emotional catharsis either at the time of assessment or in the first few psychotherapy sessions. Some of the patients who never get to psychotherapy declare it is because since they 'saw Dr Broom, I've been much better', and the above reasons are commonly the reason for this. Some are scared and do not want any more contact, and say they are better so as to justify declining psychotherapy.

Case 3

A male aged forty-two years complained of twenty-one years of pain in left shin, thigh, hip, and at times extending up his back to the neck. It all started after he got married. He said his symptoms 'strike at the heart of my enjoyment of the world'. He also complained of fourteen years of coughing, starting when his son was seriously ill. It became much worse in stressful situations. A recent serious personal crisis had led to worsening cough, chest pain, exhaustion, insomnia and suicidal feelings. All these symptoms improved with antidepressants. After a sceptical start he engaged well in psychotherapy, with therapist B, though he remained highly intellectualising. A major therapy theme was 'the extraordinary danger of revealing one's self'. He developed an increasing capacity to take risks in this respect. He rated his improvement at fifteen sessions as 40 per cent in respect of pain and 0 per cent in respect of cough. Physical symptoms exacerbated during the course of therapy were clearly related to psychological material stirred up by therapy.

This patient is typical of a subgroup of somatisers who are focused narrowly on symptom relief rather than the wider issues of personal growth. They may benefit from the early positive aspects of psychotherapy, that is, the relief of being heard, and achievement of sufficient catharsis and insight to make significant difference to their symptoms, and will often enjoy some small changes in personal functioning. They often resent the time and money involved, and make moves to truncate therapy as soon as symptom levels are tolerable. In these patients prognosis is variable. Quite a number do well for months or years but then regress and return for a further series of sessions. Many will do more definitive work with more enduring results the second or third time around.

Case 4

A girl aged six was brought for immunological assessment of one year of severe inflammatory vulvitis unresponsive to antifungal and steroid creams. She would wake her mother up to five times nightly screaming with the irritation. Routine enquiry as to whether she may have been sexually abused uncovered the mother's own experience of sexual abuse, which had never previously been disclosed to a professional. The mother had protected the child from contact with males and had also been emotionally overinvolved in a variety of other ways. In the consultation it was noticed that the child seemed unusually attuned to mother. The mother was instructed to under-respond to the symptoms and to keep a symptom graph so as to divert her energy, away from the relationship with the child, and onto the graph paper. She was never to ask the child about her symptoms but to graph unsolicited reported symptoms. The child was given soothing creams to apply, and instructed to have a bath whenever symptomatic. Mother was asked to pour the bath but to avoid all other interest or involvement. She was to give much love and attention only at times when the child was not complaining of symptoms. Three weeks later they reported that the child's symptoms ceased on the day of the assessment. Mother entered psychotherapy for resolution of her own abuse issues. The child's symptoms remain 100 per cent resolved.

Somatisation should not be thought of in only individual terms. Family therapists are very accustomed to a member of a family system expressing a symptom or behaviour which reflects something going on in another part of the system. Often it is not possible to recognise the metaphorical aspects of such expressions, or at least as easily as in this case. Other readers may wonder at the mechanisms by which such phenomena arise. Certainly this child and mother were experienced as attuned to one another in a somewhat nonseparate and entangled way rather than in the more desirable separate-but-empathic way looked for in healthy relationships. The fact that they could disrupt this so quickly is a reflection of underlying healthiness.

Case 5

A man aged fifty-four complained of nine years of severe chest, epigastric and lower abdominal pain, chronic constipation and marked hypochondriasis. He had had multiple gastroenterological interventions with no diagnostic or therapeutic resolution. He had experienced repeated 'rejection' by physicians frustrated by his presentations. Many of the symptoms and reactivities seemed to be rooted in an extremely severe rage. He was very depressed, but adamant that he was unable to take any psychotropic medications and, equally adamantly, refused psychiatric involvement. He gradually developed a very fragile engagement with me in the assessment phase, and eventually agreed to start psychotherapy with therapist H, in close liaison with myself. Early in therapy there was an early albeit slight improvement in mood, a definite correlating reduction in pain, and a perceptible increasing engagement with therapist H. A vacation period interrupted the fragile therapeutic process. Concerted attempts to get him to see a stand-in therapist over this period failed. He apparently felt abandoned, and two weeks into the vacation period he committed suicide.

A valid question here is: 'When is psychotherapy with somatisers dangerous?' Another somatising client had been fluctuatingly suicidal over a long period, and then committed suicide impulsively when abandoned by her boyfriend. Coincidentally her therapist was ill, and had been less available, at the same time. Apart from one other patient who had an exacerbation of inflammatory bowel disease whilst in therapy there have been no other patients, in the experience of our group, with really worrisome worsening of their symptoms. In Case 5 suicide had been a risk for some years. During the period prior to the vacation he was not committable to a psychiatric institution under current New Zealand law. This was certainly considered, but not only was he not committable, it was also felt that institutionalisation might precipitate suicide. Taking everything into consideration we decided to start therapy soon after initial contact, though there was a preference to do so after the vacation. Cases of this severity are very rare, in the experience of our group. Joyce McDougall (1989, p. 17) refers to the psychotic core which she postulates exists underneath many somatic manifestations. She is referring to powerful affective states and fantasy structures that are so primitive and potentially disruptive or disequilibrating for mental functioning that they must be expressed in the somatic dimension to allow mental survival. It is a profoundly important issue, because if she is right then it may be that psychotherapy will be potentially very risky for some clients in the same way that psychotherapy may be very risky for psychotic patients presenting in psychiatric practice. This hypothesis may allow understanding as to why many somatisers do not want us to get anywhere near their psychological functioning. To allow that would be to expose themselves to the terrors of an uncontrollable exposure of the inner psychotic core. Nevertheless our experience so far is that the majority of somatisers who *do* engage in psychotherapy can do so without such disintegration. This might not be the case with those who resist psychotherapy.

Case 6

A man aged sixty-two presented with diarrhoea which he first remembered occurring at age thirteen in relation to visits to the public library. Later in psychotherapy with therapist H it became clear this related to his childhood love for reading, and the fact that during the war his mother gave all his books away. His chronic four to five times daily diarrhoea developed at age thirty-three, fifteen minutes after his mother died. His psychotherapy themes included a chronic inability to express painful and negative feelings, and the need to 'control' so as to avoid being overwhelmed, and to avoid any jeopardising of relationship. Much of the therapy consisted of learning to express feelings in the context of the safe relationship of therapy. He had twenty-eight sessions in all and achieved 95 per cent improvement in symptoms.

Case 7

A woman aged thirty-two complained of four years of distressing pruritus, fatigue, myalgias and arthralgias, and headaches. Initially she was very resistant to the idea of psychotherapy but then engaged well. Underlying her somatisation was a poorly cohesive sense of self, with marked good/bad splitting. The 'bad' part (anger, hatred, rejection) was projected into the body, and then seen as bad: 'My body has let me down' (expressed with great anger). She had to work through a strong idealising transference with therapist C, and also a compliant 'good' attachment (as a defence against the core 'badness'). She had a total of ninety sessions. Her pruritis totally resolved. The 'flu'-like symptoms were 80 per cent reduced in frequency and severity. Headaches became rare and easily aborted.

Quite a number of patients end up having longer-term therapies. It is very difficult to predict who these will be. Two patients will present with similar multiple-symptom syndromes: one will be largely symptom free after ten to twenty sessions and the other will require fifty to a hundred sessions, though most people can be accommodated within a brief psychotherapy model (ten to forty sessions). The primitive good/bad splitting and the other psychodynamic aspects seen in this case would alert most experienced therapists to the probability of a need for a longer therapy period.

Case 8

A female aged forty-six presented with an eight-month history of severe nasal congestion commencing soon after a relative with a terminal illness decided to withdraw contact with her. She felt hurt and bewildered, but in view of the relative's medical state she felt unable to do anything about it, indeed not entitled to do so. This was talked through at the first assessment, and she expressed disbelief that this relationship issue could be the cause of her physical symptoms. She subsequently reapproached the relative, and also seemed triggered into doing some other useful 'feelings work' with another important relative. At the follow-up visit a month later the physical symptoms were completely resolved. No formal psychotherapy was needed.

Case 9

A sportsman aged thirty-five presented with a three-year history of numerous unexplained stress fractures and tendon ruptures. Intensive investigations, including bone density and endocrine studies, had been unhelpful. Prompted by a friend he eventually sought psychotherapy, with therapist P. After a year he was referred for a second opinion. He had done good work in psychotherapy, but the injuries continued unabated. In the assessment connections were made between a childhood experience of a fracture of the arm, and its influence on his early relationship with his father, to his current orthopaedic episodes, and it was interpreted that these episodes really constituted a present-day symbolic and metaphorical means of communicating with his spouse. A full explanation was given, and marital therapy advised, and all injury problems ceased within a month.

The full details of this case will be published in a journal article. It represents the most florid clinical example in this book of the profound connections between the psychological and the somatic aspects of our functioning. Most clinicians working within the biophysical paradigm would see fractures and tendon ruptures as mechanical problems, as entirely somatic, and that a stress fracture could not be seen as a metaphor for some emotional issue or conflict. This case raises some intriguing issues for sports physicians.

Case 10

A woman aged twenty-five presented with many complaints: ten years of migraine; three years of recurrent herpes simplex on a buttock; six months of recurrent nose, throat and ear infections, and muscle spasm headaches; and two months of epigastric pain and irritable bowel following a miscarriage precipitated by ergotamine given for migraine. The patient was clinically depressed and systematic recordings revealed a marked correlation between mood swings and symptom peaks. The use of antidepressants improved the depression, but the physical symptoms persisted. She was not very psychologically minded but engaged in eleven sessions of psychotherapy, with therapist M. The main areas addressed were appropriate feelings expression, separation-individuation issues with parents, assertiveness, and working through agoraphobic fears. At the end of therapy all physical symptoms were 80 per cent improved.

Case 11

A man aged thirty-eight presented with a six-month history of urticaria initially associated with a syndrome comprising sore throat, tachycardia, intestinal colic, mood drop and arthralgias. No underlying illness could be diagnosed. Initially antidepressants seemed to help but the urticaria persisted over the next two years, mostly as a sole manifestation but occasionally associated with low mood and arthralgias. He entered psychotherapy with therapist T quite reluctantly, presenting with a very 'intact' persona and defences. The therapy very gradually uncovered deep fears of rejection rooted in an extraordinary story of multiple family-of-origin abortions and marital unfaithfulness. The urticaria resolved as these issues were worked through, except for some urticaria occurring purely in relation to sexual intercourse. This finally settled when further conflicts between love and sexuality were resolved.

Case 12

A woman aged twenty-nine complained of three years of recurrent anaphylaxis, dermographism, and tension headaches. Careful allergy work-up failed to find somatic cause, and anti-allergics were entirely ineffective. Fifteen sessions of psychotherapy, with therapist G, revealed a close association between anaphylactic episodes and exacerbations in anxiety related to an inner psychic 'black hole', and to powerful existential themes of worth, loss of control, and 'cosmic' loneliness. The therapy focused on 'connectedness in relationship' and issues of separateness. The anaphylactic episodes ceased completely. The headaches reduced 80 per cent.

These twelve cases, and those in subsequent chapters, illustrate the clinical variety in somatisation. The physical symptomatology is extraordinarily varied. Some patients move fast in therapy but others move extremely slowly. Patients with similar symptoms may have very different underlying psychological issues and structures. There is great potential for the psychotherapy of many somatic presentations, and at times such therapy can entail serious risks.

Diagnosing Somatisation

Somatisation disorder is a psychiatric category describing patients expressing psychosocial distress in the form of bodily symptoms. In Chapter 8 reasons will be given for the view that somatisation is not only very common, but that it is also seriously underdiagnosed by psychiatrists. The real problem is how to choose criteria for a diagnosis of somatisation disorder when, in so many illnesses, we have insufficient knowledge to make a decision as to whether or not emotional factors are operative. In the Manchester Somatisation Study (discussed in Chapter 8), for example, it was required for the patient to have a diagnosable underlying psychiatric disorder before it could be concluded that the person was somatising. That is very tidy, but is it realistic? There are many somatisers who work through the underlying emotional issues and enjoy symptomatic relief, and yet do not qualify for a diagnosis of somatisation under this criterion.

The approach enjoined here is *exploratory*, constantly avoiding the straitjacketing elements of conventional criteria, which are seen as conservative and essentially dualistic in their presuppositions and assumptions. Once it is accepted that mind/body processes may be relevant to many diseases in which most clinicians would not even consider the possibility, then it becomes appropriate to consider exploration of the healing possibilities of psychotherapy in these 'unlikely' situations. Therefore psychotherapy has been offered in many cases where there is no conventionally diagnosable psychiatric condition. At times it has been offered to patients where there is no precedent for the use of such therapy. This is always done with the full knowledge of the patient that such an approach is experimental and exploratory. The presuppositional basis for this approach is the notion that it is likely that the assumptions of conventional aetiological paradigms are inadequate, and if other conventional medical therapies are not working, or are unacceptable to the patient, it may be worth trying psychotherapy.

Nevertheless it is necessary to have some justification for encouraging patients to take a psychotherapy course, apart from a vague philosophical position, and any factors which lead one to the belief that it might be helpful are spelt out to the patient. There are a variety of clinical pointers to a somatisation categorisation elicitable in an initial assessment. Not all the pointers will be found in all patients. One patient may provide many clues suggesting somatisation; another may provide almost none, and yet after discussion both patient and doctor agree together that psychotherapy is worth a trial.

How then is a basis for a psychotherapeutic approach established, beyond operating out of a simple presupposition that somatisation may be a part of almost all clinical presentations? The following points need to be considered:

1. *All the patients presented here were referred with physical symptoms or illnesses, and all but a tiny fraction of them were unaware of the possibility of mind/body factors. In this sense they fulfil one major criterion for the diagnosis of somatisation as conventionally defined by psychiatrists.*

This criterion is that the patient must (mis)attribute his illness to somatic factors (for further discussion see Chapter 8). This very aspect of the patient's presentation makes it difficult for the clinician to argue for, and for the patient to accept, psychotherapy, though it is clear that if the patient can be shown that her assumed somatic factors are not playing a role then some willingness may be engendered. But of course many conditions are the result of multiple factors and somatisation may be only one of these. Usually the argument for psychotherapy must be established upon grounds other than early convincing proof that the problem is not physical.

2. *Though patients often presented with conventional illnesses such as rhinitis or urticaria, which are normally responded to somatically, they were all looked at for associated emotional factors. A number of features would raise the possibility of somatisation.*

Some patients clearly had associated symptoms of depression or anxiety. Some had become ill at times in their lives when obviously important (and often symbolically important) and/or stressful things were going on. The two detailed case histories described in Chapters 2 and 7 are good examples of this. Others did not present so clearly with symptoms in relation to a key event but there may have been a general fluctuation of physical symptomatology in concert with fluctuations in mood or stress levels. This was often perceived at the second visit when the mood/stress and symptom graphs could be compared (see Chapter 5). If any of these pointers to emotional factors were present a recommendation to psychotherapy would be considered. It is necessary to keep in mind that physical illness is itself stressful, and the ordinary day-to-day fluctuations of mood common to most people do not necessarily constitute collateral evidence of somatisation, though many people do in fact experience physical symptomatology in relation to these 'ordinary' fluctuations.

3. *At times the language (or story) of the patients would suggest very clearly that the illness was a somatic metaphor for an underlying affective theme.*

This subject will be discussed in some detail later but a good example would be the woman with a *facial* rash who says she 'keeps a brave *face* on it'. Another might be the patients with mouth ulcers who have something important to say to somebody but cannot do so. Another might be an angry patient with a 'pain in the neck'. Increasingly, when these connections are picked up in the assessment period, these patients are encouraged through to psychotherapy. Of course many of the symbolic and metaphorical elements are not obvious until the patient is well into the therapeutic journey.

4. *There is a pragmatic and exploratory element.*

It is not possible to say that all illnesses have a mind/body element. As already mentioned, if a patient presents with hayfever, for example, and he can be 'cured' with immunotherapy injections, then that approach will be taken. Therefore where there is an orthodox and therapeutically satisfactory answer to certain illnesses psychotherapy is not usually offered. A diagnosis of somatisation does not mean an automatic referral for psychotherapy. It is important that no harm is done, and that the patient's best interests are served. Many well established physical illnesses may have a certain ongoing autonomy or relative independence of mind factors, whatever may have been the influence of these latter factors in predisposing towards or precipitating the illness. These are speculations. Generally there has been no push towards psychotherapy with patients where other very acceptable remedies are available. To do so would be to risk ethical misdemeanour. Nevertheless this posture does represent a certain falling away from a holistic paradigm. There is no need to deny the patient a collateral somatic approach. Both somatic and psychotherapeutic approaches can be exercised in concert. Up to now the work has been with patients with conditions where other remedies are not satisfactory or are not available. One exception to this is chronic urticaria where experience of psychotherapy in this condition is now so extensive that referral through for psychotherapy occurs in most instances.

5. *A small group of patients present asking for something different.*

They may have had multiple medications, consulted many practitioners, and some (patients with nasal problems for example), may even have had multiple surgical interventions. Patients with gut problems may have been investigated extensively by endoscopy. These patients may have a history of many years of medical consultation and treatment and are weary of chronic illness. Some of them will quite willingly try psychotherapy. One couple recently requested assessment, for psychotherapy, because they believed the husband's renal vasculitis exacerbations were somehow linked to exacerbations in the wife's polysymptomatology. Nevertheless, despite patient preferences, it is preferred that these patients do exhibit some of the features outlined in the above paragraphs before psychotherapy is recommended.

These are the factors which have influenced recommendation of psychotherapy to somatisers. Over time many patients have gone on to psychotherapy and done very well. A feedback loop operates. A patient with a disorder which has not to this point been approached via psychotherapy, is somewhat nervously recommended into therapy. If he does well clinical boldness develops and more patients with the same condition are encouraged to do the same. There may also be some room for extrapolation to other related conditions. If these persons do well other illnesses are considered, and so on. Strict 'criteria' determining a basis for psychotherapy have not been developed. The feeling is that such criteria would presuppose a fixity of knowledge and the emphasis has been on exploration.

Struggling with Presuppositions

Any exploration of what is often called 'the mind/body problem' involves many interconnecting conceptual territories. Inevitably one is drawn beyond science, biology and psychology, to philosophy, spirituality and sociology. These all demand some attention in the struggle to find new ways of thinking about and working with patients with illnesses which appear to have dimensions in both mind and body. Any talk about mind/body disorders is always rooted in presuppositions about the nature of reality.

   The problem of nomenclature (see below) is also ultimately a problem of presuppositions. It has been a struggle to find an entirely suitable language with which to discuss mind/body disorders or illnesses, as they are conceived here. For instance, phrases like 'meeting places between mind and body', or 'the mind/body connections', are questionable in that they presuppose a separation of mind and body, or that separate entities are coming together. This is misleading if the notion of a dualistic separateness of mind and body is a faulty conceptualisation. Chapter 9 emphasises how faulty this mind/body dualism is.

The specific interest here is in mind and body in relation to illness and disease, and, even more specifically, as seen from the vantage point of an observer/clinician who is committed to keeping both mind and body in focus at one and the same time. This commitment is maintained both initially when confronted by a person with an illness, and also as the clinician goes on to respond to the ill person in a way that is healing. This commitment requires something more than an orthodox and general acceptance of the importance of emotional factors in health and disease. It is a commitment to keeping both mind and body matters in focus all of the time. The cases offered so far hint at the fact that this approach gives rise to a quite different clinical panorama to that which most of us have become accustomed to.

This book also brings together two disciplines which usually have little to do with one another: the disciplines of internal medicine and psychotherapy. Internal medicine is a very body-focused discipline and psychotherapy is very mind-focused. They each represent professional derivatives of both sides of the mind/body dualism referred to above. The approaches of the two disciplines will be mixed quite freely.

The struggle experienced by the author in blending the two disciplines has to be, in part, a reflection of personal difficulty in transcending personal dualistic presuppositions, and entrenched habitual compartmentalisations of the various aspects of personhood. Some of this difficulty is of course entirely unique to the author, but the experience of having taught and supervised many psychotherapists and doctors, and having watched these motivated professionals repeatedly regress back into unhelpful compartmentalising and dualistic modes of practice confirms that the struggle is experienced by most Western-trained clinicians, at least to some degree. Western culture is highly conditioned to dualistic and physicalist presuppositions, and it should be expected that change in this will involve a struggle. Many readers will have inherited the powerful and pervasive legacy of scientific and medical thinking developed over several centuries, and many of the elements of this legacy are both inimical to the healing of the person and very difficult to modify.

This book, then, is for doctors who are searching for ways of bringing the mind into their soma-focused practices, and for psychotherapists who want to learn how to work with clients with physical symptoms rooted in emotional issues. It may also prove useful for lay people who are simply just interested, and for patients who are dissatisfied with the responses they get to their illnesses from professionals. It can make a great difference to a patient's willingness to engage in a new and often threatening type of therapeutic process if he or she can become sufficiently informed to feel a partner to the professional. Much of the material in this book will be accessible to intelligent non-professionals.

Of course doctors and psychotherapists themselves are also patients at times, and have their own somatisation problems. Teaching this material to professional colleagues inevitably stimulates interest in their own personal mind/body functioning. This book cannot be read as if the problem is 'over there' in the patient or the client. The mind/body problem concerns the professional personally. For this reason professional readers may be stirred and challenged and perhaps quite discomforted at a personal level.[3]

Struggling with Nomenclature

Whilst conventional disease-labelling systems are seen as a reflection of current knowledge and ways of seeing reality, and in fact play a real part in restricting how much of reality is actually seen, they are nevertheless crucial to communication, and to the systematisation of current knowledge. But from the outset it is suggested they be held loosely so as to avoid being locked up by them. The use of any term can also imply a quite unjustifiable scientific finality or precision. The truth is that no one really knows the actual limits and boundaries of expression of mind and body, but some terms are rather high-sounding and tend to

---

[3] When I give seminars on mind/body matters, and choose to lead off by telling the group about my own emotionally based symptoms of headache or neck ache (thereby giving the group permission to be open), and then ask the group to identify their own symptoms, it is rare to find an individual who does not have any. The problem we are talking about in this book is common, if not universal.

suggest that the body of knowledge is more substantial than it really is. It is hoped that readers will get a feel for the range of phenomena in which mind/body issues arise and then start to explore for themselves the extent and nature of the problem. Clearer definitions may be possible in the future. In the meantime the terms 'somatiser' and 'somatisation', as used here, seem adequate to describe a person presenting physical symptoms as one dimension or expression of a 'whole' which includes non-physical psychological or spiritual elements. Presuppositionally the author leans towards a unitary, nondualistic view of the person which allows physical, psychological, social, and spiritual elements to participate in the 'disease' process even if the main visible manifestation is in the physical dimension.

Psychiatric terms are widely utilised, and, as mentioned earlier, one of these is 'somatisation disorder' which, explained simply, means putting one's emotional responses and issues into one's body, or into bodily form.[4] Certainly this occurs very commonly and the term is a valid one in many respects, but it does tend to imply a dualistic and linear mind-into-body mechanism, as if: 'I am putting my emotions into my body; I am transfer-

---

[4] Some readers will be very familiar with psychiatric approaches to these disorders. The definition of somatisation disorder, given above, is derived from that of Kleinman and Kleinman (1985). They define somatisation as 'the expression of personal and social distress in an idiom of bodily complaints with medical help-seeking'.

A conventional psychiatric view of the multisymptomatic disorder known as somatisation disorder sees it as a rare condition, and it is hardly ever diagnosed in males. Readers might like to refer to the *Diagnostic and Statistical Manual of Mental Disorders* (DSM-IV) of the American Psychiatric Association to understand current taxonomic thinking in Western psychiatry, in respect of mind/body disorders. In five years of formal psychiatry training the author saw only one patient with somatisation disorder, as defined in the DSM-IV (1994). This is partly because they are under-represented in psychiatric practice and over-represented in internal medical and primary care clinics (for a review see Ross et al. 1995). It is claimed that the prevalence of somatisation disorder is 0.2–2 per cent in women, and less in men. But this depends upon the definition of somatisation and in turn on the presuppositions determining the definition. In this book it is argued that many people are expressing their stories in their bodies without qualifying for the psychiatric diagnosis of somatisation disorder as defined in DSM-IV.

The current psychiatric usage of the term somatisation disorder to define an extremely rare and florid subcategory is absurdly limiting.

ring them from one compartment to another.' Such linear concepts may adequately describe some situations, but the term does not adequately cover other possible scenarios or mechanisms; for example, the more holistic concept where the person not only expresses himself in all dimensions, in mind, body and action, but where, more than that, all these expressions occur simultaneously (for a more detailed discussion see Chapter 9). All conceptualisations imply more fundamental assumptions. A linear view of somatisation tends to emphasise that in certain clinical situations the mind aspect is primary, and the physical phenomena are secondary or derivative. Though this may be true in certain situations, it is a very simple view.

To some extent the decision as to whether it is the phenomenon expressed in the mind or the phenomenon expressed in the body which appears to come first in the chain of events may be determined by quite simple obfuscating factors. For instance, which experience, mental or bodily, is perceived first by either patient or doctor? Many patients find it easier to define their physical states than their emotional states. They pick up the onset of the former earlier than the latter and immediately assume that the physical symptom preceded, for example, the drop in mood. These observa-

Note 4 continued. There are compelling reasons (see Chapter 8) to believe that somatisation disorders (if we must use this terminology) comprise a numerically large grouping of clinical presentations. The current psychiatric view is a consequence of the extremely dualistic and physicalist thinking which characterises modern medicine.

The current psychiatric approach to somatoform disorders (essentially all psychological disorders expressing themselves in bodily form; somatisation disorder is seen as a subcategory within the wider grouping of somatoform disorders) does not encompass a wide variety of disorders which are considered here as appropriate for consideration in mind/body terms, for example, asthma, ulcerative colitis, apthous ulceration, vasomotor rhinitis, cancer, and so on. DSM-IV excludes from its somatoform disorder category any disease with demonstrable *organic* features. The term 'organic' implies that if you can see it, cut it out, slap a poultice on it, or measure something happening, then nonphysical factors do not need consideration. Thus psychiatry neatly defines itself out of clinical involvement with a vast array of illnesses which may have very significant mind/body connections. It is also clear that such a position is very dualistic. The somatoform disorder categories used by the psychiatrists are helpful in some clinical situations. The problem is that they are too limited, and they are not used here so as to avoid being restricted by currently inadequate psychiatric presuppositions regarding mind/body connections.

tions imply two assumptions which may be quite false. The first assumption is that body usually leads mind, and the second is that mind/body and body/mind processes are essentially linear. It is not contested that the mind-into-body conceptualisation implied by the term somatisation can be clinically useful, but it is an inadequate vehicle for a more unitary, noncompartmentalistic conceptualisation. The same can be said for the wider category somatoform disorders.

The concern here is to use terms which are as adequate as possible; terms which

- point more to the whole person than to the physical disease;

- avoid compartmentalisations, where possible;

- challenge dualistic and physicalist reductionisms;

- are big enough 'containers' for the huge variety of expressions of the person in the physical mode; and

- avoid the reductionism of idealism as a polar alternative to modern materialism or physicalism.

The author does have spiritual beliefs but prefers to embed these in the context of a concept of personhood as having many aspects, the visibility of which depends upon the position of the observer, and that a truly unitary approach must involve an honouring of all aspects. An approach rooted in idealism might see the somatic symptom as just one expression of a more fundamental underlying reality, which can be expressed in multiple dimensions or projections (that is, mind, body, action) concurrently. This implies that there is 'something' more fundamental beneath or prior to mind and body. Some might prefer spiritual conceptualisations to describe such a reality. Others might choose more neutral language. Such approaches are still essentially dualistic.

In this book the person is seen as a unitary whole without holding any aspect as primary or secondary. In this way 'experience' occurs within the whole person who does then have options as to how that experience will be expressed. It may be expressed in all dimensions or just one. Certainly some patients express themselves mainly in somatic mode and if the observer 'sees' only that somatic expression he ends up with a very restricted view of the person (see Chapter 9).

In summary the following tentative model of personhood is implicitly or explicitly the basis for the book's approach:

1. the person is unitary but multidimensional;
2. the person's experience is in the whole, though it may be seen most clearly in an aspect of the whole;
3. the person may 'choose' to emphasise one modality of expression of experience (or personal reality) over another, or it may be that some things are more naturally expressed in one dimension rather than another;
4. the person's expression of experience or reality may be unimodal or multimodal, and if the latter, then that expression may be concurrent, or, if sequential, a linear aspect to reality would appear; and
5. the person's experience includes physical, psychological, spiritual and social aspects and these are all seen as crucial to health and disease, though the emphasis of this book is more on the psychological and physical aspects of patients' stories. All such stories are being told (in this instance) to physical/psychological *observers*. They could have been elicited in such a way as to emphasise the social and the spiritual. In this view all traditional categories of personhood (body, mind, spirit) are seen as different aspects, and often concurrent expressions, of the same unified reality.

The Range of Illnesses Considered

Some readers might be wondering which diseases will be discussed here. To some extent this question is itself a product of conditioning to dualism and (either/or) mind or body thinking. Are there really any diseases which should be excluded?

The illnesses described here include:

(a) those of clear cause and remedy, for example, infections, allergic asthma, and so on;
(b) those of unclear cause and variable availability of remedy and cure, for example, diabetes, some cases of asthma, irritable bowel syndrome, eczema, rhinitis, and so on; and
(c) those of unclear cause and no available remedy, for example, chronic fatigue syndrome, some chronic headache states, fibromyalgia or musculoskeletal pain states, and so on.

The word 'cause' is used with some misgiving. Taking allergic asthma, for example, it might be imagined that the cause is known because the patient is known to be allergic to house mites. But why is this patient allergic? The allergy is partly genetically determined, and clearly also due to house mite exposure. It could be left at that. But though a lot is known about the physical factors, the psychosocial factors have not been excluded from participating in a causal way. There are few diseases where physicians can claim to know the full story of cause.

Non-medical readers will probably recognise that the categories of disease listed above more or less cover all known diseases. From a unitary point of view this book is concerned with all the categories, and, in principle, no disease is excluded from a holistic approach, including disorders with clear genetic elements. The dualistic reader may be thinking: 'Category (a) is body-only, category (c) is mind-only, and I don't know about category (b)'. The reader is encouraged to avoid such assumptions, to hold judgement, and to keep an open mind.

Factors Influencing Engagement

Over the years it has become clear that a variety of factors contribute to somatisers failing to enter psychotherapy:

1. *The initial assessment process is crucial.*

Generally speaking, somatisers are not very psychologically minded, and to get them onto a psychotherapy waiting list can be something of an achievement. Some are quite psychologically minded but cannot see the connection between their symptoms and their emotional states and are reluctant to engage in something which seems quite hypothetical. For many of these patients, going on a waiting list for therapy is an act of trust in the physician, and for some it is more basic than that, it is an act of desperation. But the goodwill generated in the initial assessment process enables the patient to step cautiously down the recommended path.

2. *The goodwill generated in the initial assessment can vaporise very quickly.*

If the patient is willing after the first assessment to proceed to psychotherapy, but has to wait for several months, then the goodwill may dissipate. For many patients the educational material which convinced them in the first place is forgotten, or goes out of focus, and the fragile motivation for therapy is eroded. Some of them have become reinvolved with their family doctor, or health practitioner, and are engaged in a further round of somatically oriented solutions and the mind/body focus starts to blur. Some have spoken to friends and relatives who have poured scorn on the somatisation hypothesis. Given these factors militating against engagement it is felt that to engage nearly 50 per cent is reasonably effective.

3. *When a therapist does contact a person to suggest a start to therapy, and to make an appointment, the way it is done can make a great deal of difference to whether successful engagement occurs.*

A therapist who is aware of the delicacy of the situation, who spends time explaining to the potential client what is involved in a reassuring way, who is experienced enough to know how to phrase explanations in a nonthreatening way, who is warm and respectful and certainly not pushy, and who offers a pilot therapy of a few sessions which the client knows he can pull out of – such a therapist will have a high engagement rate, especially if the waiting list is short and the client is invited into therapy soon after he has been assessed.

In this chapter I have attempted to set the scene for the clinical approach of the next few chapters. For readers who are keen to get on with more conceptual elements, Chapters 8 and 9 can be read prior to Chapter 2.

2 THE DOCTOR IS SILENT

For it is one of Wittgenstein's basic contentions that what is *outside* the framework of Logic, what cannot be integrated *within* Logic, is something of which we cannot even validly speak. What is outside Logic he defines as 'unsinn' or nonsense. The striking beauty of his final proposition, 'Whereof one cannot speak, thereof one must be silent', is meant to establish an impenetrable barrier, or so Wittgenstein believed, between what can be said and what cannot be said.

(Shalom 1985, p. 13; original emphases).

Scientific Method and Medical Silence

Human illness presents an extraordinary diversity and complexity. This is often managed by resorting to oversimplification and reductionism. For instance, a bacterial throat infection is usually seen as a simple matter. There is a cause in the bacterium and a cure in the antibiotic. If this is the only focal plane then the clinician can treat the patient and walk away satisfied. But why did the person succumb to the bacterium? Were there other causative factors or cofactors? Why didn't his wife get the infection? Did he succumb because he lost that building contract? Mainstream medical practitioners are curiously silent here.

Modern medicine demands research, scientific method, measurement and methodical laboratory verification of the 'facts'. Clearly such emphases focus attention on the body and all aspects of physical reality. The result of this is to downgrade realities which cannot be managed easily by the scientific method, and in the end it seems that for scientists such realities do not exist, or are neglected, or become dwarfed in importance through lack of attention. Wittgenstein's proposition might therefore be reshaped: 'Whereof one cannot *scientifically investigate,* thereof one must be silent.' Whatever ideas individual doctors may have regarding 'worlds' of reality outside the physicalist

THE DOCTOR IS SILENT

paradigm, most will conform to the prevailing mode of approach and remain 'silent'.

There are many diseases about which a great deal is known, but there is really no substantial grasp on causation, despite being able to provide very useful palliation or even healing remedies. Rheumatoid arthritis would be a case in point. Despite decades of research and thousands of research articles, mostly focused on the biological aspects of the disease, it seems that many aspects of the immunopathology are well understood, and yet the 'cause' remains elusive. In many other diseases there is a similar awareness that the cause is out of focus. This feeling may be, at least partly, an artefact of a simplistic belief in single factor causation. But most clinicians would acknowledge that the causes of most diseases are unknown.

The problem may not be so much the quality of the research work being done, but that the researchers are, in their work, largely ignoring an important segment of reality, and thereby denying themselves access to crucial data relating to cause(s). This is a fundamental presupposition of this book. Medical research (on nonpsychiatric conditions) has been powerfully productive in its explorations of many aspects of disease, within the limits of a restrictive biological model or conceptualisation. Yet many are starting to feel dissatisfied with the lack of potentiality of this model, despite the extraordinary advances of medical research in the twentieth century. It is as if we can know more and more, and again more, of the biomaterial aspects of disease, and yet causes of disease, in many instances, remain elusive. Simply stated, we should be looking in other places as well. We need to research 'physical' diseases utilising models of personhood that go beyond the restrictive conceptualisations of scientific materialism.

Psychiatrists have been espousing biopsychosocial conceptualisations in mental illness for many years now, although they have strayed from this into an overemphasis on the biological aspects of psychiatric disease in recent times. It is high time that nonpsychiatric medical practice gave more weight to the nonbiological aspects of disease.

A Case of Prostatitis Treated with Psychotherapy

The case described below illustrates and emphasises several important issues. First, the man had had multiple common physical ailments treated for many years by numerous clinicians without the mind/body aspects being suspected, let alone addressed. Second, it will be seen that there is a wealth of data readily accessible in his history which provides a persuasive psychodynamic logic for why he has developed the illnesses. Third, it provides an introduction to the kinds of emotional material uncovered in the process of therapy with somatisers. This sort of material is very familiar to psychotherapists and their clients, but may be quite novel for nontherapists. It is typical of the sort of material uncovered in any therapy of somatisation.[1]

George, a thirty-five-year-old electrician, was referred because both he and his doctor suspected his recurrent prostatitis was 'stress-related'.[2] He had had the disorder for fourteen years. The symptoms of this inflammatory disorder (of the prostate gland at the base of the bladder) included feelings of bladder pressure, pain on passing urine, pelvic and back pain, swelling of the testes and painful ejaculation. The symptoms had become much worse over the previous six months and he had been given six courses of antibiotics in an attempt to settle the problem. Interestingly, an attack of prostatitis was sometimes preceded by an acne-like rash on his face, and mouth ulcers.[3] Other symptoms experienced dur-

---

1 This first case presentation provides skeletal psychotherapeutic content and process and minimal technical and interpretative comment, though some of the material is highlighted using unexpanded footnotes. The footnotes are inserted at this stage to help nonpsychotherapists to notice interesting points which may otherwise be missed. Inclusion of these points within the main text would disturb the cohesiveness of the clinical story of the patient.

2 This patient presented differently to most somatisers in that the mind/body connections were acknowledged at the outset. Many degrees of patient insight are observed alongside the presentation of symptoms. Doctors vary in their awareness as well. In some cases both the patient and the doctor fail or refuse to recognise the connections. Sometimes the doctor accepts the connections but the patient refuses to, or the other way round! But in the majority of cases there is poor awareness on the part of the doctor and little if any awareness on the part of the patient.

3 Over the years the patient had seen two urologists, two gastroenterologists, and a general physician. There was a clear consensus that he did have a genuine prostatitis. At times haematuria had been recorded, and the prostate had been described as enlarged and tender by the urologists. Repeated urine cultures had shown no evidence of infection despite apparent improvement on empirical antibiotic treatment. The only laboratory abnormality had been a slightly low serum Immunoglobulin M level. Reiter's and Behcet's syndromes had been considered and dismissed.

ing an episode included fatigue, disturbed sleep, decreased libido, headaches, irritable and depressed mood, and poor concentration, memory and 'thinking capacity'.[4]

In addition, over the same period of fourteen years he had suffered from migraine, irritable bowel (abdominal pain and bloating, diarrhoea and constipation),[5] *and reflux oesophagitis (causing heartburn). He also had hayfever and asthma, though only to a mild degree.*

This much was ascertained on the first interview which had a predominantly medical emphasis. Nevertheless he did comment at this time that his symptoms had some relationship with 'stress', and he felt that his recent deterioration was related to the unpredictability of his new electrical business. A brief and superficial exploration of this suggested that the problem somehow related to his need 'to understand and control'. We noted this but made no serious attempt to pursue this theme into more fundamental core issues.

Over the next few weeks the allergic and immunological aspects were explored, he filled out symptom and mood/stress graphs (Chapter 5), and tried antidepressants (to no avail). Gradually, throughout this period, the multidimensional nature of the problem started to emerge.[6]

He brought his wife, Sharon, to the second interview and this proved very helpful. First, she confirmed that his physical symptoms appeared to be stress-related. Second, she said that whenever she became ill (for instance with influenza) George would almost immediately become ill as well, with his own characteristic symptom complex, as if his physical functioning was in some ways tied to hers.[7] *Third, they agreed that his symptoms began soon after the birth of their first child.*[8] *She had a vivid memory of that time, of herself standing in the hallway of their house in an acute dilemma. Her screaming infant was in the bedroom and her husband was in the*

---

[4] Most clinicians would regard these symptoms as evidence of clinical depression. In Chapter 5 the relationship between somatisation and depression is considered.

[5] At times he had had excessive rectal mucus and sometimes bleeding but after barium studies, colonoscopy and rectal biopsy the final (and repeated) opinion was that he suffered from irritable bowel syndrome.

[6] A gradual movement from a full addressing of the medical aspects to an increasingly psychological understanding.

[7] McDougall's concepts of 'one body for two', a reflection of incomplete separation-individuation, may be relevant here (McDougall 1989).

[8] Note the 'faultline' concept of the importance of life events. An event with symbolic importance opens up a faultline into very important issues, often sufficient to precipitate illness.

kitchen with a severe migraine. The dilemma was, 'which one will I go to first?' George confirmed that this was probably how it was.

They then started to talk energetically about how difficult it was for him to separate from or be free from his mother, and how much she controlled him. It was starting to become clear that his illnesses were in some way related to being tied-in to mother and this was being mirrored and repeated, in some way, in the marriage. The birth of their daughter could be seen then as destabilising this 'arrangement', or, using a seismological metaphor, as opening up a 'faultline' down into the real underlying issues.

Finally Sharon expressed fear of any psychological exploration of the underlying meaning of his symptoms, especially if it meant the uncovering and expression of anger in the relationship. They agreed that she discouraged open expression of negative feeling within the relationship, and this raised the possibility that George was using an alternative physical and illness conduit for these and other feelings.[9] They were quite unable to decide at this point whether he should proceed into a psychotherapeutic process or not, the limiting factor being Sharon's reluctance for the marriage to be disturbed.[10] They went back to the family doctor to get his opinion and then decided to proceed, and three weeks later we began the first formal therapy session starting with them as a couple.

At this first session I discerned a general sense of remoralisation, of reassurance, and a reduction of fear regarding George's physical health. There was also a sense of conviction that he was now going down the right path, and certainly a determination on his part to persevere. There was a new freedom, initiative and autonomy: 'I've got to do this psychotherapy for me.' He was able to say this somewhat angrily to Sharon, perhaps challenging any tendency in her to prevent him, and this seemed to be a specific example of a more general anger at those in his life who had not allowed him to get on and do what he wanted. We contracted to work with him on his own.

Over the next two or three sessions a lot of data were collected which helped us understand the mind/body connection patterns which had developed.[11] The important points will be summarised briefly, using his own words where it may help the reader to enter

---

9   The patient's family 'system' plays an important reciprocal role in maintaining the illnesses.

10 Showing unusual insight into the implications of therapy for these physical illnesses.

11 The data-gathering and formulatory phase.

the poignant world of a child, who became a man, who became a patient, and who eventually had the courage to sit down and look at the rich tapestry of his life and how illness became perhaps an inevitable component within the patterns of that tapestry.

George was hospitalised at age two months with a 'pituitary gland disorder' and he was 'expected to die'.[12] His mother had said 'I never expected to rear you', and the belief endured 'that this child had to be looked after especially well, and protected'. He was not particularly unhealthy through the remainder of infancy but his parents remained anxiously overprotective. He developed asthma by the age of five and this was cause for great concern.[13] His parents would often stay up all night watching him. There was considerable physical encouragement from his father but his mother limited his sport at school and controlled his diet. He remembered not being able to go on a high school field trip because 'the food might not be satisfactory'. In George's memory it was 'a normal condition to be sick' or even 'good to be sick'. At least this was his perception of his mother's attitude. She was 'the sort of person who focused on what was wrong in the body'. He could remember feelings of anxiety and happiness as a child but had very little memory of more specific negative feelings. The impression gained was that 'negativity' of the body got more acknowledgement than 'negativity' of the mind.

He was able to describe his mother more vividly than most people who somatise and are in therapy for the first time. She had been physically unwell since her own adolescence, and suffered from migraines and 'bilious attacks'.[14] He believed she had 'never been happy in her life', never satisfied, always 'looking over the fence', never at rest, indecisive, illogical, suspicious, and looking for hidden meanings in other people's behaviours and words. She often felt manipulated, never risked offending anyone, but usually 'grizzled about them' after contact. She 'controlled me almost totally'; 'she made all our decisions, where to go and what to wear'. It was as if 'we didn't know our own minds', and as if she were saying: 'I'll do your thinking for you.' Her decisions were illogical and arbitrary, and it was confusing and bewildering to be around her: 'You never knew where you were with her.' He was unable to

[12] The beginning of the very early somatic focus: the 'precipitating' event.
[13] The parents' presuppositions were 'confirmed', and the 'sick role' established.
[14] Mother's personal somatisation tendencies and soma-orientation as 'predisposing' factors for the patient's development of illness.

resist her because he was afraid of her wrath. If she were opposed she would 'tongue-lash you for days'. For him it was 'continual mental attrition', and 'I became anxious all the time.' He became very careful not to tell her what he felt and his father modelled this approach as well. 'We all still avoid saying what we think.' The anger behind this description is clearly discernible. The detail of George's expressions is spelt out so that the reader can get a feel for the actual life experiences which are translated into disease manifestations.

George saw his father's severe and undiagnosed tremor as being due to the erosive effect of George's mother upon him: 'The relationship with my mother has gradually destroyed him.'

George underachieved at primary school. Prevented from playing sport, he developed an artistic bent. At high school he did well except in mathematics; his mother said to him: 'I'm no good at mathematics, so you won't be either.' The lack of clear separateness between mother and son was only too apparent. He was expected to go to boarding school but, not surprisingly, he was unable to leave home. He had 'little to do' with the family decision to put him into an electrical apprenticeship. It was arranged between his father and the headmaster.

He was transferred by the electrical firm to a branch in another city where, separated from his family, he developed nausea, vomiting and abdominal pain. He remembered feeling intensely alone, very anxious, and a profound 'lack of ability to cope'. He was eventually transferred back to his home town and the symptoms settled.

He met Sharon and an important ingredient in his attraction to her was that 'I felt secure with her.' She was a 'dominant person like my mother'. She was highly efficient, motivated, and 'in control'. There was some comparison with his mother in that Sharon's true feelings were never clear to him, and he would find himself becoming tense, wondering 'what is wrong?' He agreed that he still felt quite hooked into her.

They delayed having children for some years so that Sharon could develop a career, but eventually a daughter was born. Though George was pleased he also 'felt shut out' and Sharon seemed 'very preoccupied'. In those days he was 'frantic in home and garden' and he had depended on the capable Sharon for help. Now he felt abandoned. Soon after the birth he developed the 'terrible back pain' which turned out to be the start of the prostatitis, though initially it was misattributed to a squash injury. The prostatitis symptoms worsened and he was off work for two months. Because of the pressure of all this the baby was cared for part-time in a creche and the relationship between George and Sharon improved, and so did the physical symptoms: 'Everything went back on an even keel.'

But the history since that time had been of fluctuating physical symptoms with some connectedness between the level of symptomatology and the state of their relationship. In part the symptoms could be seen as functioning to draw them together, as well as being indicative of lack of separateness, based on the impaired separation-individuation arising from the noxious relationship with his mother. He said that, 'When I got migraines I would not be able to drive home and Sharon would have to come and collect me.' He was able to connect that to: 'My mother would always devote her attention to me.'

At that point in our data-gathering I was convinced of the worth of proceeding with psychotherapy. I was persuaded by several factors. There was no clear medical remedy available to him. Both of us were convinced of the real connections between his illnesses and the day-to-day emotional experiences of life. Finally there were clear stories of symptoms emerging in relation to crises which themselves were to do with problems in separation-individuation. These latter would be highly accessible to therapy. George was motivated, psychologically minded and intelligent, and we had developed a good therapeutic alliance.

Some of the material which emerged during ongoing therapy and which seemed to underpin the emergence of illness, will now be described. He recalled the onset of his migraine and prostatitis at the time when the relationship with Sharon changed after the birth of their daughter, with such language as: 'You are on your own'; 'As a boy if I ever got into strife I could call to my father "come and help me"'; 'I didn't know how to cope.' When I nudged him as to what that was really like for him he said it 'was as if my wheels had fallen off'; 'as if I had hit a wall'; 'I was dangerously out of control.' Pressed even further it seemed that underneath these feelings was a vague and shadowy dread of 'total disintegration' or of 'not surviving'. Accepting this then as core emotional data it was not too surprising that such important and powerful feelings might express themselves vividly in the body, especially if there was no adequate conduit for them in language, or resolution of them utilising language.

Asked how these feelings related to his migraine and prostatitis, he said: 'I am saying: "Go easy on me, I'm not right; I'm not a well person". I withdraw to a comfort zone. They give me anti-

biotics for my prostatitis and then I decide to come out again. The antibiotics give me mental therapy – I'll be OK now.'

When asked about the difference between the prostatitis and the migraine, he said the migraine was *'instantaneous'; 'a way of turning my back on tasks and challenges when I feel I am not coping'.* But the prostatitis was not instantaneous. *'It allows me to withdraw',* and *'perhaps it is a good excuse not to have sexual intercourse'.* In some ways the prostatitis seemed to have more to do with how things were going within his relationship with Sharon, which symbolically reflected the exigencies of relationship with mother, or, more specifically, the dependency and separation-individuation issues with her.[15]

Vocationally he saw his life as having been arranged by his father and the headmaster (on top of a life arranged by his mother). There were anecdotes implying anger at superiors who stifled and contained him. Though he wanted to be free, he knew he had also resisted taking steps towards freedom; it often felt safer for him to remain with the *'institution'* and perform competently within it. It was as if he was on a branch, ever longing to fly. Eventually the branch broke and *'it was as if it was flap your wings or perish'.* So he set up his own business. Without the protection of family or institution, *'I'm naked and vulnerable',* and *'Going on my own I'm in grave danger.'* All of this was easily understandable in terms of the early experiences with his parents.

Much of this material was expressed in a rather vehement mode suggesting considerable underlying anger. But he was able to access some sadness and, elaborating upon this, he said: *'I'm afraid of being lost'; 'I don't know which way to go'; 'It's like there is an internal blackness'; 'Whichever way I go I hit a dead end ... it may be something to do with my brother getting lost once. And my brother fell out of a tree once ... .'*

The sensitive reader will capture some of the power and poignancy of these feelings and themes and, putting them in the context of his infantile illness and his relationship with his mother, begin to understand why George has experienced a pervasive sense of dread for much of his life, and perhaps also understand why this has been expressed in the body and in illness.

George had a total of twenty-three sessions over one year. The symptoms largely subsided within the first eight sessions and

---

15   This material could be interpreted in a variety of ways from different theoretical vantage points. I took an interpersonal approach, choosing to work out the separation-individuation issues in relationship with myself, in a brief psychotherapy mode.

any minor exacerbation was utilised to explore the underlying themes. At the time of writing he has been free of prostatitis and migraine for a year. Any hint of a possible return of symptoms can be aborted by him if he disciplines himself to focus on the themes and feelings emerging in his day-to-day existence. His irritable bowel has largely settled, though he did have a brief exacerbation recently prior to Christmas when business pressures accumulated and he did not have time to attend to his emotional functioning adequately. His symptoms have improved overall at least 90 per cent.

Many aspects of George's life were touched on in the therapy journey. But the main focus was the reality of his competence, and his ability to survive and survive well. Crises likely to precipitate symptoms were those that stirred up fears of loss of personal freedom, any perceived inability to determine his own channels of activity, and any occasion where he had to negotiate his separateness from mother, wife, employer and, of course, in the end his therapist.

A Personal Journey towards a Mind/Body Integrative Approach

Having introduced the reader to the basic orientation I will now describe how the clinical approach developed. This will further expose some of the implicit and explicit assumptions and presuppositions, as well as providing a critique of current conventional medical practice.

Between 1971 and 1986 I moved from specialist training and academic research to hospital consultancy practice in allergy and clinical immunology, and then to training in psychiatry, subsequently specialising in psychotherapy. I graduated from the Otago Medical School (Dunedin, New Zealand) in 1967. In receipt of a New Zealand Medical Research Council Training Fellowship in clinical immunology I spent five years in both research and clinical units in Birmingham, London and Montreal during the 1970s, finally returning to an academic and teaching position at the School of Medicine in Christchurch, New Zealand, in 1976. There I set up a hospital service department of clinical immunology.

The discipline of clinical immunology, in a hospital setting, tends to attract referrals of patients with a wide range of conditions. There are the usual allergic and connective tissue disorders, auto-immune disorders, and immunodeficiency diseases.

But of particular relevance here are the numerous disorders which do not fit tidy and conventionally labelled categories.

In 1981 I left clinical immunology and spent five years working at registrar level in the speciality of psychiatry, and finally as a consultant physician attached to the department of consultation and liaison psychiatry. In 1986 I, and several other professionals, established a medical and psychotherapy centre which includes general practitioners, psychotherapists, and myself as an allergist and psychotherapist. Over subsequent years we have developed training programmes in intensive psychodynamically oriented reconstructive psychotherapy, a specialisation in the therapy of mind/body disorders, and supervision groups for therapists and doctors interested in working with somatisers. My own personal practice developed into a mixture of consultative allergy and clinical immunology, psychiatric assessment, psychotherapy and psychotherapy teaching. At least this is how it was in the early years. I had not anticipated the impact of this mixture upon my clinical understanding and perspectives.

The Unexpected Impact of Mixed Practice

Day after day in my allergy work I found myself faced with patients who had conventionally labelled somatic disorders and yet, when looked at with psychotherapy-trained eyes, were clearly somatisers. Some had disorders with clear organic or physiological disturbance and some did not; that is, some had very clear pathology and others had symptoms that were more vague and hard to measure with the usual examination and investigative techniques. Those who appeared to be somatisers did not often fall into the clear somatoform disorder category of the DSM-IV. Many did not appear to have a psychiatric disorder at all. Examples included urticaria, eczema, rhinitis, asthma, various headache syndromes, back pain, irritable bowel syndrome and other gut symptoms, genital inflammatory disorders, fatigue syndromes, various polysymptomatic presentations, and even recurrent stress fractures and tendon ruptures. I was startled and somewhat overwhelmed by what I was seeing.

Many people come to an allergist in the hope that he will be able to find a simple and exogenous answer to their troublesome symptomatology. This expectation is often inflamed by unbalanced journalism and also by unfounded assertions made by alternative medicine practitioners who profess allergy expertise. Many of these patients are avoiding facing emotional truths, and therefore present as somatisers, and are looking for a practitioner who will collude with this way of managing the problem.

I found myself focusing upon the mind/body connections in an ever-enlarging group of patients, many of whom were not that keen to hear what I had to say. Initially I was inclined to limit these connections to a narrow spectrum of disease or illness, but that became increasingly untenable as I found myself unable to deny what I was seeing outside this doctor-chosen spectrum. Nor could I with any integrity maintain a body-only approach for the allergy patients and a mind-only approach for the psychotherapy clients. That sort of dualism had been quite satisfactory for me as a practitioner in my pre-psychiatry days but now, in terms of what I was seeing as the reality for many of these patients, this seemed to be an unethical denial of the truth, and a refusal to get involved with clinical realities that seemed very pertinent to the patient's search for healing. I started to devise efficient ways of responding to the somatisers with an approach that attended to both mind and body, and this book sets out that approach as developed so far.

Diagnostic Categories and the Untidy Margins

Diagnostic labels are both a blessing and a curse. We recognise a pattern of clinical presentation and we give it a label. Before long the label almost seems to get the status of an *entity*. We tend to say: 'He's got rheumatoid arthritis or eczema.' In reality we have labelled a clinical disturbance in the person, which we have seen often enough to recognise. The person does not have the entity called rheumatoid arthritis. The person is sick and the pattern of the sickness is the pattern we have labelled 'rheumatoid arthritis'. This might sound like semantic quibbling but it will be seen later that these differences really do matter.

I have already indicated that a clinical immunologist tends to see a variety of patients with conditions which do not fit into tidy diagnostic categories. An example might be a patient with chronic fatigue, vague joint symptoms and a low-titre antinuclear antibody, along with troublesome irritable bowel symptoms and frontal headaches. This is a symptom cluster which may push diagnostic buttons for several different medical specialities (immunologists, rheumatologists, gastroenterologists, psychiatrists). But certainly in this sort of case it can be very difficult to be sure of the diagnosis. Does this patient have a mild lupus-type dis-

order?[16] Or does she have depression, with an incidental antinuclear antibody? These are totally different diagnoses with very
different implications. That is confusing enough, but my main
point is that this patient does not cleanly fit my tidy diagnostic
categories and that makes me, as a physician, anxious. The truth
is that my diagnostic labels merely reflect my current knowledge.
In all sorts of medical clinics there are patients presenting with
'untidy' symptom clusters, and they are hard to label. They often
provoke doctors into excessive biotechnical investigations, so that
the anxiety of 'not knowing' can be relieved. These days I feel a
lot more confident in my management of such a patient, realis-
ing that out in the community there are many such patients
(with similar noncategorisable symptom clusters) and I do not
need to be driven to force the patients into one of my clear
diagnostic categories. Clinics of all specialities have many
patients presenting with symptoms or symptom clusters which
are investigated in case something serious might be missed but
for which, in the end, no explanation is found. Medicine is
much less tidy than our taxonomic systems might suggest. Over
the years I have learned that these patients with untidy
syndromes have much to teach us. The reason for this is that
they expose our ignorance, whereas the tidy syndromes merely
reflect our taxonomic methods of organising our current state of
knowledge.

Resisting the Pressure to Investigate

In hospital practice the emphasis tends to be on ruling out and
treating serious or sinister 'organic' disorders. This is a legitimate and
appropriate emphasis for many clinical situations. But the other 'hard
to define' disorders, many of which present in general practice and
specialist outpatient clinics, tend to be referred on to a variety of
specialists who investigate the problem according to the narrow diagnostic parameters of their own specialities. As a clinical immunologist I was (and still am) often at the end of the queue and found
myself in the position of saying: 'STOP – no more investigations'.

16. Nonmedical readers may have some difficulty discerning the significance of this example. It is sufficient to say that the clinical material
does not clearly fit any one of our diagnostic categories but may
suggest a number of conditions or diagnostic labels such as systemic
lupus erythematosus, irritable bowel syndrome, depression, tension
headache and chronic fatigue syndrome.

Stopping the investigative juggernaut was anxiety-provoking for me in those days. Most of us recognise the potential shame of 'missing something', and especially something serious. Shame is a powerful motivating factor in the practice of medicine. Little did I realise that in those days most of us were missing very important things most of the time. More of that later, but for the moment it suffices to say that in those hospital consultant days I was at least learning to tolerate diagnostic uncertainty and developing the courage to stop endless costly investigation. I was starting to realise that the fear of missing something, the availability of technology, the need of the patient for answers, and the need of doctors for recognition of expertise and income may all contribute to a chronic illness presentation by the patient and an equally chronic illness responsiveness by the doctor.

The Pseudo-certainty of Medical Labelling

I was also seeing the limitations of medical labelling systems. These are so essential to medical communication and research but are they always in the interest of the patient? To be able to assign such labels as 'irritable bowel disorder' or 'vasomotor rhinitis' or 'muscle tension headache' has some value. They certainly say what is *not* happening. The patient does not have cancer or allergy and also knows now that he or she fits into some 'known' category. The clinician has the reassurance that the client 'fits' somewhere and the medical literature may be able to assign a prognosis and offer some symptom-relieving protocols. But if such labels give an illusion of 'knowing' and in the end get in the way of other ways of seeing, then the doctor and the patient are colluding in a maintenance of the illness.

Technology: a Convenient Dance Partner

Another characteristic of modern medicine is, of course, its dependency upon technology. Technological investigation and treatment play an important role in most medical activities, especially in specialist clinics and hospitals, and the availability of these is significant in a variety of ways. First, technology enables the physician to make diagnoses where active responses are crucial to treatment and prognosis. But, second, in the cases where useful treatments are less available or diagnoses are uncertain, access to technological investigation can give the clinician a sense of efficacy and the patient a sense that as much as possible has been done. I will emphasise later that in many cases nothing is further from the truth. So many somatisers are repeatedly investigated over many years and the doctor/patient processes engendering this might be seen, stated rather brutally, as a collusive 'dance' of technology, of medical somatic preoccupations, of doctor/patient ignorance, and of doctor/patient avoidance of the mind/body connections. A very complicated dance.

Discovering Somatic Preoccupations

Since leaving the hospital system I have become aware of how somatically preoccupied I and my specialist colleagues were. This has some very real justification in that hospitals generally manage illnesses with gross somatic manifestations or patients with endstage disease. Arguing for a focus on some putative or notional psychosomatic substrate to these serious illnesses hardly seems relevant to a registrar struggling in the early hours of the morning with patients with septicaemia or acute left ventricular failure. It would seem even less relevant to the patient! But as I will argue it is far more relevant to the vast horde of somatisers outside the hospital system. So what is the problem with the somatic preoccupations of hospital doctors? The problem is that medical students who are trained largely in the hospital setting are therefore getting a totally inadequate preparation for understanding and responding to somatisers. I will be arguing that somatisers form a large bulk of general practice and we are sending doctors out into the community with a very limited and skewed preparation for what actually exists out there.

The Hospital Teaches Me what to 'See'

Hospitals have become groupings of narrow specialisations with a highly technological emphasis. The explosion of scientific knowledge, the advances in technology, and the proliferation of therapeutic options (often of marginal benefit) all bias towards a somatically preoccupied training experience. Individual organs are focused upon, more or less in isolation from the person as a whole. Psychosocial issues are often ignored unless the patient is unmanageable or the 'mind' issues are so grossly obvious that they can no longer be ignored and then the consultation/liaison psychiatrists are called in. This perpetuates the notion that such issues are only relevant in the exceptional patient. In my view and experience the vast bulk of the mind/body problems we meet in medical practice are more subtle.

Perhaps that statement is false to some degree. Perhaps it is not that they are subtle; perhaps we have eyes which have only been trained to see the somatic face of reality and if we looked with different eyes we would see a very different or at least enlarged reality. Many illustrative examples will be provided to support this view.

Psychiatrists are not Integrationists

I have also had ample occasion to ponder the influence of psychiatry upon this alleged somatic preoccupation of clinical medicine and medical training. My judgement is that its influence has been minimal, or perhaps we could say that psychiatry has done very little to counteract this somatic emphasis. It may even have cemented the problem into place. As already mentioned, in the early 1980s I abandoned internal medicine for nearly five years and participated in a full-time psychiatry registrar training programme. This was a fascinating and challenging experience. I gradually came to recognise some important elements in modern psychiatry bearing on why it is that medical practitioners are so ill-equipped to deal with somatisation. One of these is the question of competence. In my experience most psychiatrists feel as inadequate in matters of the body as physicians or surgeons feel in matters of the mind. Most psychiatrists do not try to act as mind/body integrationists. They sit comfortably on one side of the dualistic split. The exception to this is the small psychiatric subspeciality of consultation/liaison psychiatry. The impact of this service is small because generally it only serves the (hospital) patients referred to it by the somatically preoccupied physician or surgeon. There is great irony in this. The somatically preoccupied are allowed to circumscribe the purview of the mind-oriented when it comes to exploring the mind/body connections. In my experience the consultation/liaison psychiatrists have little passion for the problem of somatisation as it presents at general practice level and do little to impart a more comprehensive mind/body perspective to the few medical students and junior medical staff who gain access to working with them.

My comments so far have to do with the practical impact of psychiatry upon the practice of nonpsychiatric medicine in its somatic presentations. I am not at all dismissing the enormous contribution of psychiatry to nonsomatic illness and indeed to the category of somatoform disorders, though in the latter instance the work that has been done has been constrained by the implicit dualism of the psychiatric approach.

Soma-preoccupied Psychiatry

Another influential trend contributing to the failure of psychiatry to modify the dualism of modern medicine, and what stood out for me as I worked amongst psychiatrists, was their growing preoccupation with biological mechanisms. The brain is the last and least accessible body continent to be explored with the tools of biotechnology. An aggressive exploration is needed. But when I left medicine to enter psychiatry I was reaching out, as it were, from the soma across the gap to the psyche, and was disappointed to discover many psychiatrists 'abandoning' the psyche to embrace the soma, in the form of the brain and its biology. Stated as simply as this it is something of an exaggeration but certainly the burgeoning understanding of brain function and an increasingly available investigative technology has biased many psychiatrists to a 'biological' emphasis. Thus, rather like their physician/surgeon counterparts, they have become somatically preoccupied, or in more specific terms, preoccupied with brain biochemistry and structure. In some extreme cases it is as if the mind and its expressions are some sort of complex epiphenomenon of the brain to be responded to from an emotional distance and with medication. But in my experience few patients are best served by a narrow approach emphasising brain biochemistry and medication. Certainly the host of somatisers in general practice do much better if more than tranquillisers and antidepressants are available.

The Low Status of Psychiatry

Another problem has been the low status of psychiatry in the medical profession and certainly in hospital medicine where medical students develop their clinical attitudes. My experience has been that the psychiatrists by and large accept this. It has been most interesting that in recent times in New Zealand with massive changes in the health system there has been wide consultation with the community as to its health priorities. Mental health services figure very highly in community priorities and this is in stark contrast with the priorities learned in medical student training. I suspect that until psychiatrists grasp the nettle of holism and begin to be assertive about the importance of mind/body processes the somatically oriented clinicians are going to be able to continue to subordinate them. After all, 'We, the somatically preoccupied, are dealing with matters of life and death [of the body] and you, the psychologically preoccupied, are merely dealing with subjective discomfort [with obvious exceptions].' I believe this sort of dualism or 'splitting' is pervasive in medicine, and is so false as to be laughable. But it is no laughing matter. Our collusive failure to attend to the protean mind/body issues will be revealed eventually as a failure to attend to truth now generally available and this failure is indeed to the marked detriment of our patients' clinical care.

These then were the observations and experiences I brought from my research, hospital consultancy and psychiatry training days to my 'mixed' allergy and psychotherapy practice. In the early days I battled with a lot of uncertainty and experimented with a variety of approaches. I came up against many difficulties and some of these are worth describing as any practitioner attempting a combined mind/body approach is likely to experience them too.

Obstacles to Mind/Body Integrative Practice

First I observed a rising anger among patients towards the medical profession with its narrow biological focus. More patients are demanding to be seen holistically (perhaps manifest in the drift to alternative therapies), but despite this it is still only a small minority who see clearly a need for an exploration of the emotional underpinning of their physical symptomatology. Such a suggestion is often highly threatening. Many shrink away and some are indignant. Handling such responses can be quite stressful for the doctor. What sort of distorted version of my opinion will the patient take away? Will the referring general practitioner continue to send patients my way? Am I right in my judgement anyway? After all, the diagnosis of somatisation cannot be confirmed until a therapeutic response to psychological approaches is shown. This takes time and I have to endure my own self-doubt and the patient's fluctuating scepticism.

Professional Loneliness

Another struggle for me was the professional loneliness. Conversations with my erstwhile physician colleagues about mind/body issues proved very unrewarding. Responses included scepticism, boredom, polite disinterest, and for me the feeling of hopeless distance experienced when trying to communicate with another when we do not share any language. I often felt I was swimming against a very strong tide and the water was cold and dark. Gradually, however, I have found general practitioners much more responsive, and over recent years many have attended seminars, training workshops and regular supervision. I am fascinated with the possibilities for general practice as clinicians develop counselling skills and apply them to somatisation. I have found that with regular supervision doctors can acquire competent counselling skills (useful in the management of somatisers) much faster than my experience with nonmedical therapists had led me to expect.

Conventional Practice Structures are not Helpful

The therapeutic work with these patients cannot easily be slotted into the conventional ten- or fifteen-minute slot. The initial processes can be delicate and precarious. Despite these difficulties it has been most gratifying for me to watch general practitioners, fledglings in the area and starting nervously, doing excellent work and coming back enthusiastically for more skills and awareness. The training element is very important. None of us get satisfaction from tackling things we do not have the competence to handle. One of the justifications for this book stems from the pleasant discovery that it is practical to train general practitioners to work in this area.

Before I conclude this section I need to touch on alternative medicine and psychotherapy as two other areas which are relevant to the problem of somatisation.

What About Alternative Medicine?

Though all medical practitioners are now well aware of the drift of patients to unorthodox therapies, allergy practice certainly attracts patients who are looking for 'the causes' or nonmedication answers to their symptoms. One of the attractions for patients in the alternative therapies is that they purport to offer more 'natural' approaches. Nevertheless, in my view, most of the fringe therapies are as somatically preoccupied and mind-neglecting as orthodox medical therapies. For instance, in terms of my experience most of the so-called 'food allergies' diagnosed by alternative practitioners have no foundation in fact, and I have seen many people who have spent much time and money and instituted sometimes dangerous dietary approaches, nearly always to no avail in the long term. My point is this: what begins as a journey of hope away from the restricted symptom-relieving approach of orthodox clinical medicine towards an approach which purports to be natural, holistic, and definitive, often turns out to be another blind alley. Even worse, what often ensues is an entanglement in unscientific and false assumptions which are usually just as somatically dedicated as anything the patient may have left behind. In my opinion a patient on a restricted diet for an allergy he has not got (as an explanation for fatigue, myalgia or headache) is perhaps further away from resolving his anger (for instance) than he was when he was taking paracetamol (for symptom relief) even though whilst on the diet he is doing something 'natural'. On the other hand there are many alternative medicine practitioners whose therapies are highly 'somatic' but who come towards the client in a very caring and relational way, and in my view much of the good done flows from this.

The Role of the Psychotherapist

Finally I come to the psychotherapists. I have kept close company with the practice of rigorous professional-level psychotherapy over the last ten years and this has been through psychiatry training, personal therapy, psychotherapy practice, teaching psychotherapy, and constant personal supervision. I have immersed myself in psychodynamic theory, object relations, self psychology, Sullivanian interpersonal theory and many other aspects of psychotherapy. I feel as 'at home' in this discipline as I do in clinical medicine. I have discovered some important things relevant to the good care of somatisers. First, simply referring a patient with somatisation to a skilled psychotherapist who has no special expertise in this area often leads to a disappointing outcome. There seem to be several reasons for this. The therapist usually has no medical or paramedical training and lacks confidence in matters of the body, tending to skirt around somatic symptoms and often deferring to the patient's doctor who, more often than not, is somatically preoccupied and who may continually derail the therapy by further investigations or physical treatments, or just by failing to support the therapist in a mind/body connection focus. Thus the client may be tempted continually to look for answers in the wrong place. This is a collusion of forces: the psychotherapist's lack of medical confidence; the doctor's somatic preoccupations and fears of missing something; and the patient's defensive need to avoid the mind/ body connections. Thus, simply referring somatisers on to a psychotherapist is not likely to be all that helpful. In practice, although I see psychotherapists as more integrationist than the medical profession, they do in fact tend to be mind-preoccupied, comfortably occupying the mind-side of the current Western dualistic splitting of the mind/body complex. This is fine for non-somatiser psychotherapy clients but is no good for somatisers and represents a collusion with the powerful orthodox somatic focus of the medical profession. 'You do your thing and I'll do mine.'

A Workable Situation can be Achieved

At this point in time I find two situations work reasonably well. The first is where skilled psychotherapists work under my supervision. In this situation I support them in their psychotherapy, and in their focus at the mind/body interface, and I provide the medical security they need as the client continues to proffer physical symptoms to the therapist and some assessment of the medical significance of the symptoms is needed. The second situation is where I supervise general practitioners training as therapists. I am coming to the conclusion that this is probably ideal: the combination of good psychotherapy and general medical skills in the same person. But the ideal is hardly ever achievable. Good training in mind/body matters and easy access to appropriate mind/body-attuned medical or psychotherapy advice/supervision will allow most of the potential problems in this type of work to be addressed satisfactorily.

Conclusion

I have attempted to give some idea of the framework of experience within which the ideas and clinical practices proposed in this book have been developed. I recognise that these are to an extent idiosyncratic but I am confident enough now that many of them are easily taken up by practitioners of widely different backgrounds.

In the next chapter I will present a metaphor which will enable the reader to unify the somatic, psychological, and spiritual aspects of the person. It stresses that these aspects of the person are to a considerable extent only separate from one another because the observer comes to the person from separate vantage points.

3 FACING THE PRISM

Revelation ... is always mediated through symbol – that is to say, through an externally perceived sign that works mysteriously on the human consciousness so as to suggest more than it can clearly describe or define ... A symbol is a sign pregnant with a plenitude of meaning which is evoked rather than explicitly stated.

(Dulles 1983, p. 131)

Metaphors and Symbols

In medicine and psychotherapy there is a great need for metaphors and symbols of personhood, or, more precisely, metaphors and symbols to convey the depth and breadth of what is meant by personhood, and from which to expand an understanding of healing. The practice of medicine has a dominant body-only focus which emphasises the ever more thorough examination and exploration of the physical aspects of the person and his or her organs. This approach has become very atomistic. The implicit prevailing metaphor in this mode of dealing with the person is that of the 'machine'. In this metaphor the machine is opened up or taken to bits (atomised). The parts are laid out on the floor. We try and repair those parts in need of repair, and then work hard to get them all together again so that the machine can continue to function. The body is a very fine machine of enormous complexity and fascination and many of us expend most of our available energy in the various tasks created within this scientific and biomechanistic enterprise. This effort is expressed in many honourable avenues of investigation and involves much expenditure of energy and resources, and indeed much more needs to be done to understand our somatic level of functioning.

Whilst the medical biomechanics are busy 'fiddling with the machine' the psychiatrists and psychotherapists largely stand on the sidelines accepting the machine metaphor, at least implicitly.

There is very significant discussion amongst them about the limitations of current approaches to the person but the bio-mechanists are not really experiencing much challenge from the mind professionals to their machine orientation. The machine metaphor is so dominant and entrenched in our educational and professional institutions that a revolt is needed to force acknowledgement and utilisation of other more holistic metaphors.

But passive lamenting is not enough. This chapter offers a different metaphor, the metaphor of the prism, which not only permits a conceptualisation of the person as a whole (as also does the machine metaphor), but also encourages the observer to see the person from very different vantage points (the machine metaphor does not do this), and from there to respond to the person as a whole. This simple metaphor has been very helpful in our clinical work, and it seems to be a very useful one for the professional to utilise as he or she starts to practise in a more holistic way. It does have its strengths and limitations, as do all metaphors.[1] The reader might consider for a moment what the issues might be in choosing suitable metaphors.

Choosing Clinically Useful Metaphors

First, a metaphor must enable the clinician to recover that which has been lost or ignored. The prism metaphor helps regain holism and some useful integration of the parts of the person, especially the integration of mind and body. Second, it must be appropriate to the needs of the clinician and the patient in terms of their current understanding of reality. That is, there is little use in a metaphor which is so advanced that neither the clinician nor the patient can utilise it in practice. It must facilitate a movement in them towards a wider view of the person. Some conceptualisations are too difficult to be of practical use at this point in the 'hurly-burly' of the medical clinic. There are other new metaphors, such as the holographic paradigm, currently being discussed quite vigorously by theoretical physicists, neuroscientists, philosophers, and those into New Age spirituality and

---

[1] On the negative side the prism is visually bare, hardly suggesting the complex detail of life. On the positive side it is a simple container for the enormously complex unitary elements of personhood which must be imagined, implied and evoked rather than obsessively captured in the perfect diagram.

the eastern spiritual traditions.[2] The holographic paradigm is of great interest. Very simply, Bohm (see Chapter 9) argues that the stable, concrete realities of persons and the world are in a sense illusory, and emerge from a more primary order or energy field called the holomovement. Pribram (1985) adds to that the notion that the brain's mathematics comprise a 'lens' which makes concrete objects out of the holomovement frequencies. These notions are very provocative, and stimulatory to holism, but hardly useful at this point in the clinic explaining somatisation to patients. The last point should be qualified. The holographic paradigm is present in the clinic, implicitly present in my understanding, and because of the presuppositions brought to my work. It is there within and affecting my own ever-changing presuppositional processes. But it is of no use yet as an educational tool for engaging patients in a journey of integration of mind and body as they struggle with their illnesses and symptoms. Perhaps one day we will have patient populations who are educated to new ways of seeing reality so that other metaphors, currently thought of as gobbledegook, may become more accessible.

The third consideration then, in choice of a metaphor, is that it needs to be reasonably simple and yet capable of containing enough of reality, and it needs to be able to be presented to the patient or client very quickly with a reasonable hope of acceptance. The metaphor chosen is that of the prism.

Deeply Entrenched Dualism

In the struggle to discover practical ways of working therapeutically with somatisers we are confronted with our own presuppositions regarding the mind/body connections. Experience with teaching mind/body medicine shows that most doctors and psychotherapists are very surprised at the depth of their own dualistic presuppositions. Unfortunately it seems that most clinicians operate from

---

[2] Wilber (1985) states: 'the holographic supertheory says that *our brains mathematically construct "hard" reality by interpreting frequencies from a dimension transcending time and space. The brain is a hologram, interpreting a holographic universe*' (p. 22; original emphasis). Basically this paradigm blends together new understandings of physical reality derived from post-Einsteinian physics and modern concepts of brain functioning. This is hardly material for the 'common man', acculturated in a Newtonian paradigm, in a rushed medical clinic.

presuppositions which are profoundly constraining in terms of what they allow themselves to see in their patients. It seems that most just passively absorb these presuppositions by living in a Western culture and by passing through educational institutions presuppositionally working out of dualist and physicalist presuppositions. This absorption is of course largely unwitting, and until the presuppositions are challenged most people have little idea how entrenched they are within them, and even less idea as to alternatives.

I am going to introduce readers to new presuppositions but do not expect them to accept these without adequate justification. I hope to provide this as this chapter and the rest of the book develop. To help us get into the centre of the issues quickly I am going to describe how I explain to patients what I mean by somatisation, and I will do this using the metaphor of the prism. This should help the reader to get some feeling for my basic orientation without having to wade through a set of protracted preliminary arguments. I am confident that many readers will find this helpful and will be able to 'join' me earlier than may have otherwise been the case. This confidence grows out of my experience of the favourable response of many patients, doctors and psychotherapists who have found the prism metaphor understandable, respectful of reality as they see it and very practical in the clinical setting. I am going to write without restraint in the first person, because my use of the prism is an expression both of concepts and of that which is needed in relationship with this patient.

Drawing the Patient as a Prism

At some stage early in my encounter with the patient I invite him to lean forward as I draw a prism in front of him, and this allows him to experience himself emerging, as it were, on the paper before him as a multifaceted or multidimensional person. In a visual way I am asserting that he is a unity with many aspects to his reality. I could of course tell him that I see him as a biopsychosocialspiritual unity, or as a hologram, but this seems to have less than optimal impact!

Most patients seem reassured when I am not responding to them in a reductionistic way, and the simple visual impact of the prism seems to provide this reassurance. It is interesting too that the very act of drawing a diagram freshly for each patient seems important. I suppose I could have a large professionally drawn poster on the wall, and then, conveniently and easily, I could trace its elements with a pointer. But, for me, the freshly drawn prism is a symbol of the patient's individuality. It underscores his uniqueness. A poster on the wall emphasises universality, rather than individuality, and the patient is at risk of getting lost in the endless stream of somatising humanity passing through my rooms. By attending to such details I believe we are being deeply sensitive to fundamental issues of the experience of personhood, and this sensitivity is probably as fundamental to the art of healing as anything else we might do (this is expanded upon later). For these reasons the next few diagrams will be developed as the patient experiences them: hand-drawn and fresh for him.

The Patient Joins the Metaphor

Figure 3.1 shows the simple prism. It pays to stop and ask if the patient recognises the shape. The occasional patient, usually a person carrying underlying issues of control or obsessionality, will have problems with the prism. He or she may see a person as having more than three dimensions! I will go with that. There is nothing sacred about my prism, and the art of healing will always be derailed if the clinician and the patient engage in a power struggle.

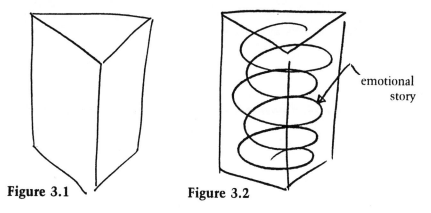

emotional story

Figure 3.1   **Figure 3.2**

The 'Emotional Story'

I then draw in what I call our 'emotional story'. I might say to the patient: 'Within all of us there is an emotional story. Some of it we are aware of but much of it is out of sight.' Clearly the term 'emotional story' is hardly rigorously descriptive. The word 'story' seems to connect with the patient's sense of longitudinal and meaningful history. Most patients recognise, to some degree, its emotionality. I am really emphasising the nonphysical story aspects of the person's reality and this can include the spiritual as well. But 'emotional story' is an approximate term which most people understand and can relate to. Figure 3.2 shows my rough representation of this 'emotional story'. Most people unhesitatingly accept this as a simple starting schematisation. At this point, because the patient has come presenting the somatic and the physical, it is my task to put the 'story' aspect into the field of view. But I have not, by doing so, pushed the physical aside and made the story primary and the physical secondary. It seems that human beings of all philosophical vantage points readily concede the importance of the 'emotional story'. For some this story may be seen as having purely psychological elements, and for others both these and also spiritual elements. In this sense the prism metaphor is pragmatically inclusive of people with a variety of philosophical positions. The person is a unity, and it depends upon the vantage point from which one looks (and with which set of spectacles) as to what aspect of the person we see. Do we, at any moment in time, see the somatic, or the psychological, or the spiritual aspects of the unified reality of this person?

Unity and Multidimensionality

My prism metaphor is not perfect. It does not express some aspects of personhood at all satisfactorily. But what it does express quite emphatically is our unity and our multidimensionality, and, as we will see, it has the power to illustrate the ways which we must find and utilise to express our psychospiritual reality. With somatisers we have to underscore these unitary and multidimensional aspects of personhood if we are going to achieve a good therapeutic result. Having said all this, let us return to the patient who at this point is cheerfully accepting the prism and the 'emotional story' as meaningful for his reality as a human being.

I then focus on some content in the emotional story. I keep it simple and mention various affects, making sure that I choose both positive and negative examples, such as joy and anger. In somatisation we are ultimately most interested in the negative affect states and themes, but to focus on only these at this stage is to invite defensiveness. I declare that in one way or another these affects will be expressed in some dimension of the person. I choose as an example the least threatening dimension first. Figure 3.3 shows a projection from one of the faces of the prism.

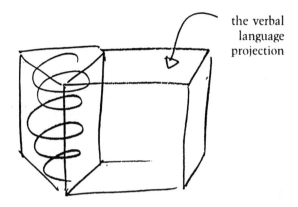

the verbal
language
projection

Figure 3.3

The Verbal Language Projection

I always start with the projection of verbal language. Joyce McDougall, in *Theatres of the Body* (1989), has stressed the importance of emotion being 'recognised in a symbolic way ... within the code of language which ... [allows] the affect-laden representations to be named, thought about, and dealt with by the mind' (p. 28). Expressing feelings in verbal language is an essential element of much of the therapy of somatisers. We want to enable the sufferer to deal with the inner pain in the verbal language projection as expressed in Figure 3.3. This of course can be extremely difficult for some patients, the most extreme group being the alexithymics who appear to have no words to describe their emotional states. But when I draw the language projection for patients I simply say that this projection is the word or language vehicle for emotion. A simple example is: 'I am angry' (expressed with some vehemence). Most of us know something of how valuable the clear verbal expression of a feeling to a responsive 'other' can be. Of course this language vehicle is no simple option, but tackling the complexities of such expression of feelings comes later in the therapeutic journey of the somatiser.

Sometimes I will embellish the prism with an extra detail as seen in Figure 3.4. I suggest that the psychiatric physician is, on the whole, looking at *patterns* presenting on the face of the

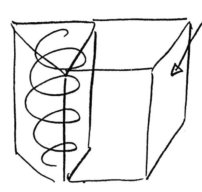

taxonomic
patterns
recognised by
psychiatry,
for example,
anxiety disorder

Figure 3.4

language projection. The anxious patient describes with words his feeling states (and other aspects of his subjective experience) and, if they 'cluster' in a certain recognisable pattern consistent with conventional taxonomies, the physician will declare the condition to be an 'anxiety disorder' (or, in the case of other patterns, schizophrenia, or bipolar affective disorder, and so on). These are 'superficial' patterns which play an important role in labelling for communication, prognosis and choice of therapy. But, in my opinion, they are not very helpful in accessing the core emotional states giving rise to the language-described symptom clusters. For instance, if one makes careful enquiry regarding the fundamental feeling states of a suicidal patient it is easy to gain access to powerful affects of powerlessness, utter isolation, worthlessness, guilt, and so on. This is the core experience of the depressive. At a more superficial level he might say he is feeling suicidal, or has no energy, or that he cannot cope, or that he is extremely anxious, or that he is ruminating constantly. These and other symptoms are typical of the symptom cluster we recognise as diagnostic of depression, but they are in the end derivatives and consequences of the underlying powerful core affects.

It is noteworthy, too, that psychiatrists have largely confined their practice to the verbal language projection, and usually profess little confidence with the somatic projection (see below). The origins of this rather constricted focus on the verbal language-described mental states have been clarified by Goldberg and Bridges (1988). They argue that, whereas in the nineteenth century the concepts of neurosis, hysteria and neurasthenia were physical and psychological manifestations mixed up together, in the twentieth century, beginning with Freud, the purely psychological pathological states (such as anxiety, phobias, obsessional states) became the main focus of the psychiatrists. The more somatic presentations (for example, angioneurotic oedema) were left to the somatically oriented physicians, and this has largely been the case throughout this century. So the practice of medicine is very definitely split with the mind and body emphases kept well apart. The physicians even removed the 'neurotic' element from the term angioneurotic oedema. As an allergist I find this deeply ironic: about 70 per cent of my cases of chronic 'idiopathic' angioedema (and urticaria) are due to somatisation and respond rapidly to good mind/body-oriented psychotherapy. But historically the psychiatrists gave up the territory and the physicians erased the role of the mind.

But these matters are hardly the concern of the patient on his first introduction to mind/body matters and usually I will not mention the role of the psychiatrists whilst I am describing the verbal language projection, as any such mention may frighten the patient and precipitate disengagement. At this point the patient is only mildly interested, has no idea where I am heading, and certainly no clear understanding of its relevance to the entirely somatic (sic) condition with which he has presented.

The Action Projection

I now draw another projection, as in Figure 3.5 (overleaf). This represents the action or acting-out projection of emotional expression. For instance a patient may say in response to a question about low mood that: 'I do not allow myself to get down, I keep myself busy.' In emphasising this projection I might mention that people have various ways of dispersing emotional energy. They might use exercise, alcohol, drugs, work, hobbies, sex, or anything of relevance to the patient. I am careful to mix together the 'good' and the 'bad' categories in a nonjudgemental way and also to list a variety so as to universalise this projection. This allows the patient to feel part of the human family rather than singled out and exposed in his possible weakness. But I do not spend much time with this projection. I mention it to honour the reality that the patient is a 'whole' and that to ignore a large chunk of him is dishonouring. Moreover many patients readily acknowledge the truth for them of the acting-out projection, and the growing conviction that I am describing their reality prepares them for openness to what I have to say about the somatic projection. The use of the term 'acting-out' may seem to suggest to some psychiatrically informed readers that I see this projection as entirely defensive. This is not so, but I do believe that, inevitably, many of our activities have defensive elements, and also that action is a valid conduit for dispersal of emotional energy. It is when it becomes a mechanism for emotional expression and yet fails to resolve adequately a troublesome core issue and also takes on self-harming dimensions that the defensive element becomes most obvious.

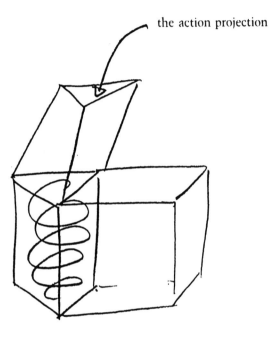

the action projection

Figure 3.5

The Somatic Projection

I now move to the somatic projection, as in Figure 3.6. It might seem that progress to this point has been rather laboured and slow: in fact, in the clinical situation, with a few well chosen words and a rapid drawing, it all takes only a minute or two.

By now the patient is familiar with my logic. But, for many, the thought that somatic symptoms might be a legitimate expression of emotion is bewildering. This issue is dealt with in Chapter 4. But, in using the prism metaphor, a typical presentation may be as follows:

'On this side of the prism we have another aspect of ourselves into which we can put our emotions. The body or the soma – we call it the somatic projection. Some of us are very aware that if we get tense we get headache, or backache, or a "funny tummy" – or indeed a whole variety of symptoms. Other people are a bit

the somatic
projection

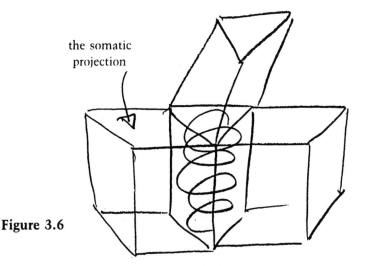

Figure 3.6

*surprised that their symptoms may be due to connections between
their emotions and their body. If I get anxious, and am too busy to
work out what I am feeling, I tend to get a tight head. If that
happens I try and stop and ask myself, what am I really feeling
and why? I don't always find it that easy but if I can identify the
feelings and work them through I find the tightness goes away.
One of the problems is that when we go to the doctor he asks us
very carefully about the symptoms – and so he should – that is
good medicine. He looks at the pattern of our symptoms and he
makes a diagnosis and we need that. The label is often very helpful. But sometimes our labels are quite frustrating. For instance,
this tummy problem of yours. It has been called "irritable bowel".
That is not telling us very much. In a large number of conditions it
is as if we as doctors are dealing with patients at this face of the
somatic projection. [I cover up my diagram leaving only the face
visible; see Figure 3.7.] Most doctors do not look at the connections*

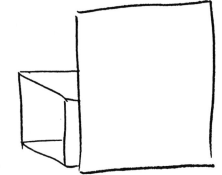

Figure 3.7

*between my symptoms and what is going on within me. [I pull off
the cover so the patient can see himself as a whole.] It may be
that there are no such connections in your case, or that the connections are too hard to find, but if they are there and we could
find them and deal with them then we have the opportunity of
making a real difference to your symptoms. It may not be relevant
to you but if we don't look we won't know'.*

This is, roughly, my approach to this projection and, of course, I
vary it according to the circumstances. An intelligent enquiring
patient may need more detail. A suspicious patient may need me
to stop and work out the fear that is blocking our interaction. A
more simple person may need simpler language and less information. The clinician must sense what is needed and what is honouring to the patient's current reality.

I have described the simple framework within which I operate
when working with patients. The prism metaphor has some drawbacks and not the least of these is that it is merely a way in which
the reality of a person can be visualised and explained simply to
patients. The notion of a single unity with different 'faces' or
aspects still seems to imply a residuum of compartmentalisation,
and I remain unsure as to whether that will remain justified in my
thinking in the longer term.

Conclusion

I would prefer a metaphor in which I was aware that I was facing
physical, psychological and spiritual aspects of a person's functioning at every given moment. I could perhaps envisage a metaphor of
coincident planes, which might suggest that in facing a person I
am in fact facing all the planes, whether I can see them or not, or
whether I choose to focus on them or not. My feeling is that
patients would find this sort of conceptualisation or metaphor
rather difficult. One of the reasons compartmentalisation and excessive dualism thrives is that we are limited in our capacities to
hold too many things together at once. It may be that the prism
metaphor is useful because it bridges the gap between two very
different ways of seeing the individual: between dualistic compartmentalisation and integrative unification. This means then that the
metaphor is really only useful insofar as it leads the observer to
some truth about reality, and continues to serve as a useful tool for
an observer who needs to develop new ways of observing. It can be

discarded easily when the observer has matured in his observing to the point that the metaphor itself has become a constraint.

As mentioned earlier, I am excited by the holographic paradigm as a metaphor upon which holistic practice could be built, but the use of this metaphor or model of reality is confined to rather advanced thinkers in science, philosophy and medicine, and is not yet able to be used in the clinical situation where one is dealing with patients and clients who are deeply submerged in old ways of thinking. For the moment the prism metaphor is a satisfactory compromise and a bridge across which people can move as they start to see themselves in different ways.

In practice I do not confine the use of the prism metaphor to working with patients I have diagnosed as somatisers; the reason being that as I go on I am no longer sure who is a somatiser and who is not! Most patients benefit from the chance to see themselves holistically. And there may be somatisation present where I have not yet seen it. I have now moved to a position where I always look for mind/body connections in all conditions. The psychiatric label 'somatisation disorder' implies for most of us that there is a distinctive group of conditions that are a somatic expression of core affective states and a large majority that are not. I would now question that. I believe that that assumption arises from a disastrous splitting of mind and body which pervades medical practice. The more one looks for connections the more obvious they become.

4 THE INTIMATE DOCTOR:
Diagnosis and Engaging the Patient[1]

> ... *intimacy*, that special dimension of relatedness which most defines the climate of psychoanalytic change. Intimacy, in this sense, may be considered the ambience of engagement or closeness between therapist and patient which characterises the 'positive therapeutic alliance' – that state of good intent and hard work without which no degree of virtuosity nor depth of experience of the therapist can prevail.
>
> (Levenson 1974, p. 359)

If doctors were trained with as much focus on relationship issues as on biotechnical aspects of disease, the positive impact of medical practice upon the health of the population would be enormously increased. An understanding of the subtle issues arising moment by moment in the doctor–patient encounter can be crucial to a successful therapeutic engagement, and a passage through to a healing outcome. Skilful psychotherapists assume the need to acquire and utilise such understandings, and in psychotherapy training a great deal of attention is given to the 'process' of the relationship transacting between therapist and client. On the other hand some doctors are rather intolerant of questioning of their interpersonal style as relevant to the healing enterprise.

Intimacy Skills

Intimacy skills are of crucial importance in the management of somatisation. There are a variety of ways of conceptualising intimacy, but here I am talking about the intimacy skills of:

(a) sensitive awareness of my own feelings, and of the patient's feelings;

---

[1] Chapters 4 and 5 are an expansion of a previous article: see Broom (1990).

(b) willingness to wait for the other person to become 'ready' (and yet avoiding collusion);
(c) willingness to go 'near the edge' in the relationship;
(d) willingness to confront (whilst still supporting);
(e) clear recognition that there are indeed two people in the room;
(f) deeply respectful assertiveness; and
(g) acceptance of the reality of conflicting agendas and choices, with the possibility that that which is good cannot be achieved, and that the 'other' is in the end free to take an unhealthy course.

These skills are integral to the practice of good medicine and the management of somatisers, just as they are integral to all healthy intimate relationships. It is very easy to list them but they are not uncomplicated skills. In fact most psychotherapists struggle greatly to polish these aspects of their functioning in relationship. I wonder if there is any medical student in the world who was ever exposed to training in these skills in any systematic way during medical school training? Most of us stumble along through our formative years haphazardly acquiring a motley collection of intimacy skills, which enable us to get through life one way or another, but which are not necessarily optimal for the delicate 'negotiations' needed in the more difficult areas of medical practice. And managing somatisers is one of those areas. Enabling somatising patients to move to a place where the engagement with the doctor or therapist could be characterised as one of 'good intent and hard work', where it can be truly said that a good 'therapeutic alliance' has been achieved, is no simple matter. I want now to tackle systematically the skills of early management of these patients.

Presuppositions in the Initial Assessment

The first issue facing us is the patient's agenda in visiting the doctor. This is a very complicated matter and we should expect both overt and covert agendas, and also that the agendas will be determined by both conscious and unconscious issues. It is so easy for us to take the observer position and talk about the patient, and the patient's agenda and presuppositions; this would be a typical relational posture in medical practice. But in fact there are two people in the relationship and the doctor or therapist has an equally complex (and, often enough, inappropriate) agenda and presuppositional contribution.

Let us clarify this problem by asking some questions. If the patient is somatising, what right have I to challenge that? If this is the person's preferred mode of defence, might I not be just stirring up trouble by exposing the emotional underlay? On the other hand, if the illness is in the form of a somatic metaphor, and is therefore a statement about an underlying reality, to what extent is the patient actually trying to communicate, and, perhaps, waiting for someone to listen and understand? Or is this somatic metaphor really just a vivid, albeit indirect, conduiting of 'energy' which has to be expressed in some way, but is not necessarily an invitation extended to the clinician to dig underneath to find the real truth? If a patient comes to me with symptoms based on somatisation and I respond to him on a purely somatic basis, am I being collusive or compassionate, or both?

I cannot accept a widespread tenet of many psychotherapists, which is that the client will start to work on his or her underlying issues when ready. In my view this is a naive form of humanistic idealism narrowly relevant to a fraction of psychotherapy clients. It is also a very convenient presupposition because these are the clients who are the easiest to work with. In my experience very few somatisers would ever start a journey out of their somatisation unless exposed to the educational and facilitative resources of a clinician who really does understand mind/body processes. Recently I surveyed by questionnaire a group of patients who had been referred to me by their doctors, diagnosed as somatising, and who had subsequently undergone and completed psychotherapy. One of the questions asked was how he or she felt about the initial assessment with myself. The following comments are typical, and illustrate the 'readiness' of the patient for a psychological view of their condition prior to being exposed to the educational experience of consulting myself:

Enlightening. Stunning too. I was shocked that I had no allergy, but then it made sense ... I knew straight away where Dr Broom was heading. In a way it was almost a relief. I still found the initial assessment a little frightening, probably because I had to look so hard at myself in front of a stranger.

Very difficult. Did not feel this counselling could possibly cure my rash. Dr Broom talked me round to try this method!!.

A shock, I had not realised or considered that my problem was anything other than physical.

We were surprised by lack of evidence of any food allergy. It took time to adjust our thinking on this matter. We were both relieved and confused and we decided that we trusted Dr Broom enough to follow his advice.

Good, but as a lay person I felt he got into the counselling side quickly ... meaning when you feel it is a food problem or something tangible and then you get told, no, the best way to fix it is counselling ... this gives you a very uncertain feeling of the future ... you just can't fix the problem by taking the 'food' away ... you have to have counselling ... it makes you think that you may never become healthy again. But he was very thorough, and I felt comfortable with him.

So out of it ... Don't remember clearly. OK I think. Was scared though.

Truly amazing that Brian Broom was able to get to the bottom of my problem. I must say it did blow me away somewhat. But for that I would give him a 100%!

Great relief at telling someone about a situation and having both that feeling of relief and other feelings accepted as valid. Appreciation of having psychotherapy explained to me ... I realised I needed help, and here was someone explaining to me that I would also have to be working hard, it would not be given to me, this was a new experience ... a welcome one, having some degree of control.

These comments underscore many issues in the initial management of somatisers, but they make clear how often patients come to their doctor with absolutely no idea of the emotional basis of their symptoms, and most are unlikely ever to discover this without help. They need help to become 'ready'. If my view is correct, that medical clinics are littered with unresolved somatisation disorders, then I do not think a passive waiting for patients (stuck hopelessly in a morass of somatising defence, of personal ignorance as to the mind/body connections, of society-wide scientific materialism, and of medical practice which 'rewards' somatic presentation) to get started on their own journeys of healing is a clinically viable or even ethical posture for a medical practitioner.

There are many other issues which emerge as we face this question of whose agenda we should attend to, or the question of what the real agendas are behind any clinical presentation, but I will try and spell out the presuppositions and principles I take into a consultation, and how in a practical way I resolve the problems which occur when there is a clash of agendas in a way which is respectful of both the patient and myself.

Truth and Freedom

A fundamental principle which I have found to be true in helping somatisers is succinctly stated in the New Testament: 'the truth shall set you free' (John 8:32). Whether the patient wants to discover the truth, or could indeed bear it, is another issue. Moreover, if McDougall (1989) is right, and that underneath some forms of somatisation there are primitive 'psychotic' emotional structures, then the discovery of the truth by the patient without appropriate clinical 'holding' and skill, on the part of the doctor, might be quite dangerous. Certainly what is ruled out here in my approach is an arbitrary and insensitive clinical attitude which bluntly informs the patient of the truth. On the whole such blunt approaches do little except to alienate the doctor and the patient. Nevertheless, as one of my psychotherapy supervisors once remarked: 'At some level all of us want to be known even though we may defend furiously against it.' If somatisation is a defence then we should expect ambivalence, that is, both a desire to be healed and a resistance to an uncovering of the underlying conflictual structure. That ambivalence is very clear in some of the quotations just given. If we are right in all this then there is no place for formulated doctrine as to whether one should or should not go for the truth underlying somatisation. Permission to do so grows out of the patient's sensing that here is a clinician with whom it would be safe to go on a journey of healing. Again that issue of safety is exemplified in some of the quotations above. I believe patients sense this safety rather intuitively and it is probably true that, in intimacy terms, many of us are not actually safe enough for the patient to proceed.

I assume then that at one level or another all patients want to be free of their disorders. That desire may be deeply buried but I believe the desire to be 'free' is universal. The disparaging comment heard so often, that 'he doesn't really want to get better', has no place in my practice. Of course there are the well known issues of secondary gain but that is the nature of emotional defence. The patient defends himself against the 'intolerable' by setting in place structures that are not ideal but are actually adaptive within the patient's total economy, and we should expect resistance to any change in this. I may be imprisoned and long for freedom, but also be terrified of venturing out into a wider world. There may also be some comforts in the prison cell that those of us outside may scorn as objects to be clung to, but this may be very understandable within the patient's perspective. Nevertheless I remain convinced that deep down all patients have a need to be free.

Patient Ignorance

The vast majority of patients presenting to a doctor appear to have very little mind/body awareness and most have come to expect a highly soma-oriented response from medical practitioners. The clinician working in this area faces some irksome ironies. Many patients are becoming increasingly dissatisfied with the typical medical symptom-relieving approach and want to know the 'cause' of their illnesses, but if one starts to approach the underlying (emotional) cause some get alarmed and perhaps even angry. In contrast a clinician with good mind/body skills will frequently find that many patients respond with intuitive resonance to a holistic formulation. Handling these variations is part of the art of healing in this area. In my view any lack of the required skills is a matter of medical ignorance, incompetence and ethics.

Two Sets of Data

In every interview I expect to look at and listen to the patient with two sets of eyes and ears. I focus on both the presenting somatic reality and the emotional underlay. In fact, as we shall see, if one actually listens to the simple things that the patient drops into the interview one can get very important clues as to the underlay. Over time I have become more radical in my thinking and it is no longer appropriate for me to assume that some patients are somatising and others are not. I no longer know where to draw the line. I would challenge the medical profession that we can no longer assume that most disorders are purely somatic. Maybe some leg fractures can be seen that way! Certainly many conditions can be responded to in a purely somatic way with a very satisfactory outcome, and I am happy to adopt a functional and pragmatic somatic approach in many conditions. But there are many conditions which remain mysteries and I endeavour to remain attuned to both somatic and other realities in these conditions. I believe that we all need practice in looking and listening in ways that may help us pick up all aspects of reality in our patients.

Respect for the Patient's Reality

Every interview is underpinned with the utmost respect for the patient's reality. This means that in some appropriate and skilful way I will:

(a) assess what he wants;
(b) introduce him to the contrast between symptom-relieving and cause-finding approaches;
(c) attempt to excite curiosity and interest in seeing his illness more widely;
(d) engage him in an exploration of the underlying realities;
(e) never force him to proceed;
(f) proceed at a pace that is both comfortable for the patient and enables progress;
(g) at every point negotiate the next step with the patient so that he remains in control; and
(h) try and judge the delicate balance between the need for the patient to be informed and the danger of disengagement if given too much information too soon – the balance between 'confrontation' and 'holding'.

In all interviews we should assume we are faced with the meeting of two individuals and, in certain respects, different value systems: mine and the patient's. At times in the history of psychotherapy practice, therapists have deluded themselves that they can practise in a way that is essentially value free. This is a myth. Values are implicit in all that we do. The respectful way is to acknowledge that reality, leaving the patient or client free and empowered to make choices as to the path he wants to travel. The dilemma is of course that we may know the path the patient must take to become free, but he does not want to take it because he is frightened. If I can ease his fear he may choose to proceed. Clearly the issues of choice and freedom are deeply embedded within the context of a deeply respectful and trusting relationship. Basically then we are working with the challenge of building a relationship in which the truth can be uncovered and worked out in a healing way. Our traditional medical approaches are often inimical to this process.

Process Rather Than Event

My approach to the patient sees my encounter with him as a journey rather than as an event. Of course many patients hope that the visit to the doctor will be a one-off 'fixit' event. But successful working with somatisation requires not just a consultation with the medical equivalent of a car mechanic, but the development of a trusting relationship in which the patient gradually becomes enabled to acknowledge the (perhaps unpalatable) underlying truth.

Structuring Practice to Suit the Problem

I need to structure my practice to accommodate this way of working. Traditional short appointments may serve the traditional somatic model (and the doctor's income needs!) but are inadequate, especially for those unskilled in the mind/body area.

A Multifocus Approach from the Beginning

The usual pattern amongst doctors, even those keen to work in a mind/body mode, is to take a somatic approach first, and if that does not work, only then to wonder about psychological factors. Clearly there is a sensible pragmatism in this. I want my possible melanoma excised, or my streptococcal throat treated with antibiotics, forthwith; any musings about antecedent factors or somatic metaphors must wait. But I believe it is possible to be clinically appropriate and expeditious and still keep in focus the somatic and psychological realities. For me it has been a matter of training myself to think widely each time I see a new clinical situation. I do not need to think in a body-then-mind sequence: why not both at once?

Furthermore, with which patient will I go on to consider psychological factors? Should this merely be defined by my ability or inability to offer a satisfactory somatic remedy? If a patient's asthma can be controlled with steroids then can I reasonably ignore the mind/body factors? Should I consider these only when I am stuck? Certainly this is a common medical behaviour. If an urticarial rash, to take a very simple example, is fundamentally due to anger but can be controlled by long-term antihistamines, I may have a sense of efficacy in the sense that I can relieve the suffering and the drugs will do no harm over the long term. But the patient is stuck with the medication, and the unrecognised anger. In my value system, seeking causes is a priority and, in my experience, many patients are also motivated to seek cause as well. I consciously own that and declare it in some way to the patient but remain sensitive to a patient's reluctance. Some patients clearly want only relief of suffering. Handled well, many patients will opt for seeking cause as a priority.

However, the biggest factor deflecting doctors from a mind/body approach from the beginning of their relationship with the patient is the assumption that most illnesses do not have a nonsomatic contribution. Most doctors would recognise many headaches, some musculoskeletal complaints, some gut conditions, and a variety of other conditions, as having some relationship with the psyche, or emotional stress. Many would be familiar with the fact that conditions such as urticaria, eczema and asthma, for example, can be exacerbated by emotional states. But most general practitioners, otolaryngologists, and ophthalmologists would not know that rhinitis and conjunctivitis can be caused primarily by depression, or other underlying affective states; or, furthermore, that these patients often do not recover unless these states are accessed and resolved. So the issue here is the lack of awareness of the doctor. I want to offer two examples in illustration.

Case 1

A forty-eight-year-old-male was referred with a ten-year history of perennial symptoms of profuse nasal catarrh, congestion, sneezing, and also 'cold, wet eyes' (rather than the more typical allergy symptoms of itching, redness and lachrymation). I could find no evidence of allergy by history, skin testing, or dietary approaches, although several ear, nose and throat specialists and ophthalmologists had declared the symptoms as allergic. I was intrigued by the term 'cold, wet eyes'. The symptoms began just after he left his wife. We explored this and found that he still saw her and did gardening tasks for her even though he had a new partner. Clearly he had not truly separated from her (in an emotional sense) and within the first session he was quickly able to express his sense of failure and sadness, at losing her, and his continuing longings for restoration of the relationship. He went on to have some psychotherapy and the symptoms resolved. This is an example of a steady stream of patients I have seen with rhinitis and conjunctivitis who are 'crying, without crying'. When I suggested this to the patient he grasped it gratefully, as entirely accurate, almost as if he had been waiting for someone to clarify the reality. In passing, note the importance of the patient's description of his symptoms. The phrase 'cold, wet eyes' gave me the clue to the underlying affective state. The more I go on the more carefully I listen to the patient's choice of words which so often reveal the real truth.

My point here is of course that the appropriate response to the patient grows out of a lively awareness of the mind/body connections. The current materialistic emphasis of medical practice precluded a number of medical specialists responding to this patient appropriately.

Case 2

A twenty-year-old diabetic male was referred (somewhat in desperation) for investigation of possible food allergy as a cause of brittle diabetes. In the previous year he had had many admissions to hospital with diabetic precoma or coma, and septicaemia, and had had a rather hopeful tonsillectomy as a way of controlling repeated systemic infections thought to be originating in the throat. Other clinical features included chronic unexplained cyclic early-morning vomiting, allergic rhinitis, problems with sedation and 'moodiness' (attributed to antihistamine drugs), chronic headaches, nightmares, and nonattendance at work for months.

In the initial assessment, I:

(a) diagnosed significant grass allergy;
(b) respectfully acknowledged the family's food allergy hypothesis;
(c) instituted a brief trial of an elimination diet (partly based on some positive but probably insignificant skin tests);
(d) identified features of depression (disturbed sleep, chronic tiredness, 'hopelessness', and perhaps the early-morning vomiting);
(e) paid understanding attention to the continuing demoralisation (due to the life turmoil and deep uncertainty about his health and life);
(f) identified very significant father–son conflicts and overprotectiveness (clearly obvious in the session and contributing to the depression); and
(g) asked him to keep symptom and mood/stress graphs (see Chapter 5).

Education, explanation, and reassuring holding was the emphasis of the session as well as some nudging to enable the father to become less anxious and therefore less protective, thereby enabling the son to separate-individuate, with a consequent rise in mood and therefore moralisation, and improvement in physical health.

He returned after four weeks asserting that he did not have food allergy and was eating a normal diabetic diet. He was now clearly identifying his mood states and their underlying causes; he was hopeful and certainly no longer depressed; all vomiting had ceased. At eight weeks he remained well and had even endured a short episode of gastroenteritis, with minimal perturbation of diabetic control. He remained well and returned to work.

This is a much more complicated case than the first but it demonstrates the power of moving from a purely somatic orientation to one that holds mind and body together from the beginning. It demonstrates the benefits of a sustained dual clinical focus by the clinician. I accept that many clinicians may find this case intimidating, in what it would require of them, but with willingness and time the skills can be acquired.

Recognising and Exploring the Psychosomatic Element in the Early Phase of the Interview

Though the clinician may assume the high frequency of somatisation, the patient usually has no idea that this is the doctor's position. We must avoid clinical behaviours which engender patient defensiveness. Occasionally I fall into the trap of assuming patient openness and have stated my position openly too early with disastrous effects. An example jumps to mind as I write. Recently a mind/body-oriented doctor referred a somatising patient to me stating in her referral letter that the patient recognised the contribution of emotional elements, had done considerable work in these areas and would be very open to my way of working. I relaxed my style and referred to my orientation very early in the interview, and to my surprise the patient became alarmed, defensive and angry. Two days later I received from her my first letter of complaint for three years. There were several reasons for this but it was a salutary reminder that somatisation is a defence, and defences only come down in a context of trust and mutual respect. These latter ingredients are developed gradually through the length of an interview and must not be assumed too early.

Some readers may wonder at the ethics of a patient going to a doctor in cases where the doctor's orientation is unknown to the patient. My approach might, at worst, be seen as a seduction of the patient into a mind/body paradigm. My counterargument is that there is a society-wide entrapment within a hopelessly narrow biomaterialistic paradigm which in many cases keeps people ill. Moreover those of us working in the mind/body area have to work extremely hard and respectfully to assist people who, for both personal defensive reasons and because of societal conditioning, are terrified of looking at the emotional underlay. It is not as if people can be sucked easily into this new approach. Usually patients move cautiously and sceptically, and make active choices, having been exposed to the uncertainties of all the options. I will leave the reader to ponder further the ethics of intriguing patients into an exploration of their mind/body connectedness.

Let us take the simple condition of urticaria again. More than 50 per cent of chronic cases are 'idiopathic' and in my experience due to emotional factors. But it would be clumsy medicine to state this outright early in the assessment. Most disorders in medicine have a multifactorial causation and urticaria is a good example of this. The mast cells in the skin can be degranulated by nervous system mechanisms, pressure, heat, food chemicals, medications, and in the allergic varieties by Immunoglobulin E-mediated mechanisms on exposure to allergens (though this latter mechanism is less common in chronic urticaria). So there may well be important somatic factors and the clinician must handle these well, and be perceived by the patient to be handling them well; the latter element rapidly increases trust. Acknowledging the prevalent somatic orientation of patients, it is helpful to gain their confidence by exploring the somatic factors first. I know that only very rarely will skin testing in chronic urticaria help me to manage the problem competently. But the patient assumes it will. If I do it and show negative results the patient is more free to give up his (false) assumptions regarding the usefulness of skin testing. If I don't do them on principle, as a waste of time and resources, I may well now have a patient who is suspicious of my competence, and this will provide additional reason to resist any mind/body hypotheses.

I always take out an elaborate history which tends to focus on the somatic first but encompasses a broad spectrum of factors. For example, for a patient with rhinitis I would normally explore seasonal and perennial factors, irritant and vasomotor factors, hormonal factors (relationship to menstrual cycle), and food and drug-relatedness. This establishes a very clear interest in the somatic. Nevertheless my ears are open for psychological data. The patient above who talked about 'cold, wet eyes' caught my attention. The patient with a headache who says that it feels like his head will 'explode' may be inadvertently referring to pent-up rage. Some years ago I heard Ed Levenson (Director of the Sullivanian Institute of Psychotherapy, New York) say that the essence of psychotherapy was to find out in what way that which the client is saying is actually true. I believe we need a good dose of that in medical practice. We need to listen very closely to the nuances of meaning conveyed in the patient's descriptions of his symptoms.

It is usually appropriate to ask casually and disarmingly whether the symptoms are ever related to stress. Avoid deep and meaningful tones and looks as you do this! The response to this question can be extremely useful in terms of gauging how sensitive or defended the patient is in this area. Flat denial might suggest that subsequent exploration must be pursued delicately. Open acknowledgement might suggest that a very direct approach would be well received, but if the clinician gets too enthusiastic he may find that the patient gets apprehensive and starts to withdraw.

The great majority of patients have made no connection between their symptoms and mood or stress states. Most of them have not even thought to look at these aspects. Others are so out of touch with their emotional functioning (as one would expect in somatisation) that such connections cannot easily be made. So in many respects it is not possible to decide on mind/body connections from the untutored patient's testimony in an initial interview. Finally, because most conditions are multifactorial the contribution from the emotional aspect may be heavily obscured by the 'noise' of other factors. For instance, the role of certain foods in irritable bowel syndrome, or allergic and irritant factors in asthma, may greatly distract from important emotional factors. Therefore early on in the interview, despite having utilised general and unthreatening questions about mood and stress, the mind/body connections will still be obscure.

Specific Psychological Enquiry Without Causing Alarm

In keeping with standard medical practice, it is important to go through the past history and family history, casually asking about physical and psychiatric disorders (in that order) without appearing more interested in one area than the other. Many somatising patients have a lifelong history of illness and the same pattern may pervade the extended family. Patients will give selective 'renderings'. For example, a patient will mention that he had undiagnosed abdominal pain at age eight, but not that he hated school; or that he had 'migraine' at age thirteen, but not that father left home that year; or that he is worried about his tender cervical glands that seem to go up and down, but not that some twelve years ago when he was eleven his grandmother discovered a large submandibular gland and panicked, surmising it was cancer; or that he seems to have had many more 'colds' over the last three years, but not that his moods have been fluctuating, and so on – the variety is almost infinite. But how does one obtain such data?

The standard symptom enquiry is an excellent next stage. I have taken out the initial history and now screen all systems as taught at medical school. Too many practitioners skimp here, and certainly many specialist physicians will enquire carefully only in their own speciality focus. But although in allergy practice I have little interest in, for example, the genitourinary system, I always enquire about it. Anxious patients may have frequency of micturition. Though the presenting somatisation may be in the nose, the patient may also get vulvitis or dyspareunia as part of a wider tendency to somatise. She might also get cardiac palpitations and musculoskeletal chest pain. I am able to pick up a general tendency to somatisation, and at the same time establish my right to ask questions in all areas of the patient's health. Thus proceeding I eventually come to psychological enquiry which, for me, includes (apart from a welter of physical symptoms) enquiry regarding sleep (initial insomnia, restlessness, dreams and nightmares, early-morning wakening), appetite (anorexia, bingeing), energy, motivation, enthusiasm, concentration, memory, problems with thinking, mood, and sexual interest and performance. Again this is done quickly and purposefully, but not with great intensity. At this stage it is part of general enquiry and the interview should not turn into a psychiatric assessment. These questions, and further questions arising from the answers given, should uncover tension states, panic attacks and depression. Throughout this enquiry (as at all times) one should be constantly on the alert for an increase in defensiveness, monitoring this as a determinant of how far one should go at this juncture, or how delicately one should proceed. It is better to draw back temporarily than have the patient disengage in alarm.

By this stage I am often starting to get a clear indication of the role of psychological factors, but it would usually be unwise to propose any such view at this juncture. In terms of the context in which I am working, that of specialist practice, the patient may be beginning to engage but there is a good way to go yet. In the general practice setting very different issues of pace arise, and the doctor may have to use the principles I am enunciating with quite different emphases. First, the patient may have seen his doctor many times in the past, and now the doctor is planning to take a mind/body stance for the first time. So the doctor is now about to change the 'rules'. I would approach this problem in a number of possible ways. I might admit to being somewhat dissatisfied with the patient's progress and suggest we sit down for an extended period some time and start again 'from scratch', taking out a full history and reviewing everything, and in effect setting up a process akin to that which I am describing in this chapter. Even just a simple review of the clinical history followed by some of the steps described in the sections below may be enough to shift the emphasis. The issue for the general practitioner is not so much that of establishing initial trust but that of changing orientation without eroding trust.

Returning to the assessment interview, it might be clear, by the time the psychological enquiry is completed, that the patient is quite psychologically minded and open, and has a ready acceptance of the notion that many disorders are multifactorial and that psychosocial factors are important elements to be considered. At this stage the patient might be asked quite directly whether there were significant life events operating as stressors around the time the disorder began.

My favourite way of approaching this is to ask: 'What has been the most important, or major, or difficult [give the patient different types of "handle" to hold onto] thing that has happened to you over the last two years [assuming for example that the patient's physical symptoms began eighteen months ago]?' This is an extremely useful question which time and time again unlocks a door into the patient's problem area. The use of just the words 'difficult' or 'stressful' will be acceptable in patients who can tolerate admission of certain levels of difficulty or stress in their lives. But many patients and indeed doctors come to such admission with reluctance, and the process can be eased by more acceptable words such as 'important', 'significant', and 'major'. Let us say, for example, that I have used the statement: 'What's the most difficult thing that has happened to you over the last two years?' A defensive or determinedly positive patient (is there a difference?) will often quickly retort: 'There hasn't been anything really difficult', or, 'My mother died but we coped with that pretty well.' I will then back away and say something like: 'For most people [here I am universalising and normalising] a

death in the family is a very *important* [rather than the threatening word *'difficult'*] event. Tell me what it was like for you.'

Often enough, if one listens clearly to the words used as the
patient describes the events, one can come quickly to a conclusion
as to the real feelings generated in response to the events. For
instance if, in the above example, the patient says: 'We coped
pretty well', I would tentatively read that as: 'We found it hard, but
overall I am pleased that looking back we have survived it as well
as we have.' I may be wrong in this 'reading' but it is safe to
assume that the verbal offerings are the audible tip of the mental
(cognitive and affective) iceberg. Quite simply, we just do not listen
to our patients carefully enough, in my experience. We also do not
put enough significance on trivial events. A good example of this is
seen in the following case.

Case 3

*A sixty-six-year-old retired librarian with many interests and hob-
bies, and apparently enjoying life to the full, and ostensibly with
reasonable emotional equilibrium, presented with a six-month
history of very severe urticaria and angioedema, at times affecting the larynx and unresponsive to a wide variety of treatments.
Her presentation was so disarming that I pushed away notions of
psychological aetiology, but after six months of getting nowhere,
and several hospital admissions, we did a one-hour psychological
exploration, which uncovered a rather unexciting irritation towards her elderly mother for refusing to wear her hearing aid.
This 'trivial' piece of information connected with a lifelong history of nonassertiveness towards her mother (the patient was
unmarried and had always lived at home). She confronted her
mother who proceeded to wear the hearing aid, and the urticaria
disappeared the same day. It returned six weeks later when the
mother lapsed back into not wearing the hearing aid and the
same remedy worked again.*

I feel very strongly that as doctors and therapists we tend to come
to the patient with our own notions of what is important and thus
miss the trivial or unimportant material, which is in fact truly
important. We must therefore listen carefully to the words the
patient uses; not only the words but also the tones used; not only
the words and tones, but also the 'trivial' facts.

Our discussion centres around how to fathom the connectedness
between life events and the onset of symptoms. One further useful
approach is to employ the term 'stress'. I must confess to a preju-

dice against this word, but do concede its validity in some circumstances. It is valid because it is a useful euphemism with which to engage patients who prefer to externalise their problems. It is also valid in that many circumstances (loss of financial security, for example) are very stressful, and often truly external in that they are events coming upon one from the outside. But many events are in fact stressful because of the way the patient perceives them, and his own self in regard to them. To continue to perceive a problem as an 'external' stress is often to perpetuate an underlying helplessness or powerlessness, or alternatively it is a way of denying his own vulnerabilities. Nevertheless, early on in my encounter with the patient I may indeed use the term freely with the patient acknowledging to myself that the use of it is in fact a way of joining the patient where he is at the moment in his approach to his problem. The patient may in this way accept the invitation to explore the stresses, and quite willingly look back over his history, and uncover meaningful associations with the death of a relative or a redundancy from a job. Unfortunately these people are usually only able to relate things to major events recognised by everyone as stressful. As I pointed out above, much of life is stressful because of 'trivial', powerfully symbolic and internally determined issues.

Other patients, whatever their circumstances have been, will be quite denying of stress. Even if there have been very significant life events, they will minimise the importance of these and discourage further enquiry. Careful clinical observation helps the clinician to avoid asking these people questions that are too direct or threatening and likely to cause disengagement. These patients are of course very likely to be somatising if they have to resist emotional acknowledgement and expression so strongly.

Gentle Education is Very Important

I would now say, after ten years of welding together various approaches to somatising patients, that education of the patient or client is one of two crucial keys to being able to work successfully with these people. Over recent years I have been training psychotherapists to work with somatisers and, just before I sat down recently to prepare a paper on the subject for a conference, I went to two of them and asked what they felt were the crucial things they had learned as they struggled to gain competence in the area. One quickly said that the thing which made a difference for him when therapy got hard was 'continuing to believe in the mind/body connections'. The second, equally quickly, said 'education' was an important factor. Actually the two principles are intimately related. The issue of education is very important because, first, if the patient is unaware of the connections, and, second, if the doctor or therapist is also shaky in his awareness of the connections (or belief in them) then the possibility of successful therapy is remote. How then can we go about educating our patients or clients?

Let us explore the elements of education by taking a typical patient presentation in an allergy clinic (but I hasten to say that the principles I emphasise are applicable in many situations). I am confronted with a patient with severe rhinitis, who has had many medications, seen several ear, nose and throat specialists, had some nasal surgery, and has been treated with homeopathy, diets and acupuncture. I might say to the patient that a possible reason the symptoms do not settle down is that there may be a number of factors driving them (*educating about multifactorial aetiology*: too many patients are looking for THE answer, a one-stop 'fixit' mentality).

I explain that there might be perennial allergy due to the house mite, and there might be food chemical nonallergic hypersensitivity (due, for example, to benzoates, both naturally occurring or added to foods). These mechanisms might be enough to make the nose over-reactive to irritants and vasomotor factors (now I am *educating the patient about the normal complexity of life and disease*; these are things the patient has always known but no one has ever spelt out).

It can be emphasised that the nose is a very emotional organ. In fact what I will often say is that many organs express our emotions and some of us tend to express them in one organ in preference to another. Many will express them in several systems (and I might describe a patient with tension headaches, irritable bowel, and seborrheic dermatitis – depending upon examples I have seen over the last few days). I also say that although the physician might treat all the allergic and hypersensitivity factors, if significant nervous system factors remain then the interventions at the purely somatic level may not be sufficient (*educating the patient about the mind/body connections whilst still maintaining the importance of the somatic*). Therefore it is very important for me to know about any nervous system factors (*educating the patient that the clinician wants to look at these factors but only in the patient's interest, and is not preoccupied with them to the exclusion of other factors*).

It might be useful to give a clinical example at this point to emphasise the multifactorial nature of disease. The case I will then present will be just one of many which might be used to educate a patient at this point in the interview whilst he is still poised wondering if my approach is valid. It is important that the doctor develops a dossier of educational cases to be pulled out and offered to the patient. It is quite remarkable how often a story about another patient (with identifying details removed, of course) can catalyse a willingness in my patients to face their own issues. Often I have chosen a story quite intuitively and found that the patient in front of me has in some respects a similar story, and, seemingly with enormous relief, he is emboldened to share it. Be that as it may, pertinent case illustrations of people I have seen in the past in which I stress their 'normality' or universality, and which emphasise the connections between their 'life' and their physical symptoms, can be very compelling for many patients.

I usually begin with an example similar to that which the current patient is presenting and will often widen it to perhaps two examples. But watch for any anger which some patients, who feel you are wandering too far away from their reality, may start to experience.

Case 4

A twenty-four-year-old technician presents with chronic asthma and persistently low peak flow rates around 200 l/min. Initial allergy testing showed significant house mite allergy. Mite reduction measures, in conjunction with a diet excluding chemicals such as benzoates, salicylates and azo dyes, led to peak flow levels around 300 l/min. She was asked to keep three-times-daily mood/stress and peak flow graphs from the beginning. As the effects from mite reduction and diet steadied out she started to observe definite drops in peak flow rates (as much as 100 l/min) coinciding with drops in mood and preceding menstruation (at which time her mood was low also). The mood graphs and clinical history suggested a covert background depression and antidepressants were prescribed (and she also started psychotherapy, but not with myself). Two months later she reported steady peak flow rates around 400 l/min, a doubling of her previous chronic baseline function, without any changes in her medication.

This sort of story could be told with little modification to any asthmatic. My intention in story-telling is to intrigue the patient into a journey of exploration as to how things hang together for *him* rather than to find a case which is exactly similar. Some similarity is usually helpful, but too much similarity can be dangerous.

Before we go on let us sum up the lessons from this case. First, it is a sound basic assumption in clinical medicine that many problems are multifactorial (readers will tire of my emphasising this). Second, where there are multiple factors it is often difficult to perceive or identify the role of any one individual factor. In this case it was difficult to see mood-related peak flow drops until the other factors were dealt with. Third, it is naive, or perhaps arrogant, to assume that because one cannot see something it is in fact not there. I do realise there are reasonable constraints to that piece of logic, but in multifactorial conditions the specific effects of individual factors overlap each other and therefore their very existence may be obscured and ultimately denied. This, I believe, has been the fate of mind factors in disease. Fourth, we must avoid an either/or mentality in this and every clinical case. This case is a clear example of the benefits of a both/and approach. Fifth, it is crucial that both the clinician and the patient are willing to look very carefully if they want to detect the mind elements. Ultimately both must be willing to see what is there and what is not there.

Let us now return to the practicalities of the assessment interview. At this point in the interview there may be some hesitancy on the part of the patient. 'What is the doctor really saying?' 'Is it all in my head?' 'Does he think I am pretending or imagining it?' Many patients have picked up this impression from previous doctors. I will often pre-empt the patient's reaction by saying: 'I wonder whether in raising the question of stress you really feel I am sort of implying your symptoms are not real, or are all in your head?' The patient will often nod agreement, and underneath be rather angry about previous experiences in which he has endured such devaluation. I get angry about it too so I have no difficulty in expressing my anger at a practice of medicine which acknowledges back pain due to a prolapsed disc, but devalues back pain due to muscle spasm due to anger. That is often the very example I use to express this point.

If the patient is concerned about the connections being made he might react by saying: 'But I am not under stress', or, 'I am a coping sort of person', or, 'I have my bad days like everyone else, but I don't get depressed, I'm not that sort.' At this point lots of reassurance and education are needed. This is how I often go about it: I tell him that modern medicine has dealt with the body as if it were totally separated from the mind and spirit, and I usually hold my two hands in the air widely apart to illustrate the separation. I then say that most of us realise that that is nonsense and that the mind, spirit and body are a unity, and I bring my hands together –

intertwining my fingers as a visual representation of the relationship of unity of these aspects of our person. Often the patient will immediately nod knowingly, as if this is something that he has known all along and is reassured to have articulated.

If a patient is clinically depressed, and may warrant antidepressants, then it may be helpful to choose a true example of the same medical condition where another patient's symptoms finally remitted under the influence of antidepressants. For example, in allergy practice I see a trickle of patients with chronic noninfective conjunctivitis who do not have an allergy, do not respond to antiallergic medications, and yet respond remarkably well to antidepressants, or more commonly, psychotherapy. Many of them on closer inspection are actually clinically depressed.

The point of all this is that the type of anecdote or other educational material chosen should help the patient feel a number of very important things. First, he needs to feel that he is not some sort of oddity, and that other patients do suffer from similar sorts of processes. That helps him get away from the feeling that he must be some sort of 'nutter', or alternatively a 'fraud' or 'malingerer'. Second, he should begin to feel a real sense of hope based on precedent given in the anecdotes. Third, the sharing of a variety of anecdotes, all of them slightly different, allows the patient to see that although there are other people in a similar situation to himself, each one of them is uniquely different. This helps him to feel that he is not being squeezed into a common box, with a consequent sense of loss of personal validity and individuality.

In this chapter I have dealt at length with aspects of the initial transactions between doctor and patient. In the next chapter we will look at practical ways of exploring the mind/body connections so as to establish greater confidence that somatisation is in fact the problem that we are dealing with.

5 PATIENT 'WORK-UP'

> I was brought up, as I suppose every physician is, to use placebos,
> bread pills, water subcutaneously, and other devices acting upon a
> patient's symptoms through his mind.
>
> (Cabot 1903, p. 344)

Unless we self-consciously reflect on our spontaneous, habitual or
automatic approaches to patients we will sometimes act unwisely
and be unable to further the healing cause. We often resist such
reflection because changing our patterns creates difficulties for us, not
the least being an unpleasant sense of incompetence, clumsiness or
uncertainty.

The material I am presenting is not a new efficient 'recipe' for
dealing with somatisers but, rather, a 'smorgasbord' of ideas which,
with practice, have very practical utility. They have become, for
me, a 'way of being' with these patients. Quickly and intuitively I
call on these resources, and within the space of a few minutes I
have interacted with the patient in such a way that many of the
intimacy and educational issues that I have outlined will have
surfaced and been faced in some appropriate way. The rather prolonged spelling out of the process here, in this and the previous
chapter, is not a reflection of the pace of the clinical process. With
practice it can become a seamless (albeit at times tense and stressful) natural negotiation characterised by interpersonal sensitivity
(on the part of the clinician).

So far we have dealt with issues of intimacy, discussed clinical
attitudes, and described important aspects of education of the patient. We have alluded to the importance of history taking. There
is nothing new in that except that I argue that the patient's precise
words proffer a goldmine of useful information to those 'who have
ears to hear'. But good mind/body medicine is more than all this.
We must hold on to that which is good in our soma-oriented
tradition. We must not forget to investigate and we must not miss
illnesses that will respond to 'somatic' therapies. The great risk of
enthusiasm for a 'new' conceptualisation of disease, or a different

mode of therapy, is that we plunge ahead in the new direction eschewing the 'old', perhaps thereby putting our patients at risk by depriving them of the benefits of the old.

Doing Things, and Soma First

What then should we *do* with our patients? If the patient is very defensive, it will have been unwise to take him as far as might seem implied in the previous chapter. Some of what I have outlined could be utilised in a second visit. In most patients it helps a great deal to explore the somatic aspects first. In this way we are relating to the patient within the framework of the dominant biophysical paradigm. Whilst this is happening the patient has time to learn trust with me as a clinician. Time and again patients complain to me that previous doctors did not examine them properly or do certain tests. I know full well that often enough the doctor is refusing to do these things because she does not believe they are worth doing, that is, they will not reveal positive findings. But in my view they are often worth doing, the reason being, first, that the patient's medical acculturation tells her that this doctor is competent if she behaves in certain ways. This is the patient's reality and we are not likely to win the patient over if we disregard it. Second, there is a certain amount of traditional magic in examination and laboratory investigation. However unnecessary it may be in some circumstances, until our attitudes to somatoform illness change I am going to continue to use the 'magic'. Of course I am not suggesting that all examination and investigation is in this magical category.

An example of what I mean might be a patient who is referred with a firm diagnosis of irritable bowel syndrome, and the question for the patient is whether allergy plays a role. Specialist gastroenterologists will have labelled the condition, and, typically, I will have concluded that allergy will not be playing a role (judged by the history, and so on). Nevertheless in this case I will personally examine the patient's abdomen and will also do prick skin tests for allergy. These are almost certainly not necessary (from my point of view) and yet they are easy to do, relatively cheap, and, in most cases, greatly facilitating of the passage of the patient to a new way of seeing her illness. Certain doctor behaviours engender trust.

This is difficult territory. Is the doctor, who knows better than the patient, arrogantly playing along with the patient until the latter is won over? Or is the doctor trapped by the patient's presuppositions and has to play along until the patient sees she can be trusted? This ethical dilemma has its origins in our assumptions about healing. Benson (1995) suggests that, after Koch and Pasteur, medical practice assumed that specific causes led to specific diseases for which specific treatments were the reasonable response, and I would add the corollary that therefore these latter specific treatments are seen as the only ethical response. The growing specific and physicalist treatment focus led to a further decline in interest in placebo and mind/body factors. So we get to the point where my performance of skin tests on patients where I know the tests will be negative, but where the patient will be reassured or satisfied in a way helpful to a healing journey, is seen as unethical because our paradigms do not include nonspecific aspects of healing.

If a patient comes to me with symptoms suggestive of an irritable bowel and has not been investigated for inflammatory bowel disease or neoplasia I would regard appropriate exclusion of these and any other serious somatic condition as a priority. In addition, every speciality has its own 'magic': allergy has skin testing, cardiology has electrocardiography, gastroenterology has endoscopy, and so on. These may be used as specific diagnostic aids and as reassurance for the patient, but I do not, in general, approve of the use of invasive or very costly investigations as clinical 'magic'. Nevertheless on occasions an expensive investigation like a Computerised Tomography Scan may be quite decisive in freeing the patient to look at the psychological element. Indeed it may be that the major stumbling block is the doctor's fear that she is missing something and, in this situation, investigations have their main role in reassuring and freeing the doctor to turn to the mind/body possibilities.

This means then that in many patients some 'unnecessary' investigations will be done. Are they really unnecessary? The clinical aim is 'conversion' of the somatising patient from her somatic preoccupation to a psychological orientation. This 'conversion' is essential to her healing. Failure to take into account the need for a gradual conversion, and a gradual building up of confidence in the clinician, is to fail as a clinician. Too many people are condemned to a continuing 'somatic' illness because of a tactless clinician who essentially conveys the message that it is 'all in the mind'. Once again let me reiterate that somatising patients 'need' their somatic hypothesis, and will only usually relinquish it in response to patient understanding and gentle nudging from the clinician, who is prepared to wait and allow trust to develop. After all, the patient has 'chosen' a somatic expression of her emotional state because it is too difficult for one reason or another to face it more directly. With appropriate encouragement many patients will face that state, but blundering tactlessness tends to increase defensiveness and locks the patient into the somatic expression.

Ideally we should be able to make a positive diagnosis of somatisation without unduly pushing the soma aspects. A patient came to me with fifteen years of fatigue, fourteen years of fluctuating nonspecific dermatitis, and a ten-year history of abdominal discomfort, bloating and vomiting. It was very clear from the outset that the symptoms correlated with the difficulties of her marriage and her pattern of interiorising negative affect. She had had a 'gut full' of stepping carefully around her volatile needy husband. She was ready to hear a psychological interpretation and start therapy forthwith. She had had various investigations over the years with little benefit. She was quite happy to discard her misattribution of symptoms to food allergy. I ascertained that there had been no fundamental change in her physical symptoms to suggest that something sinister was developing which might benefit from a specific therapy (such as surgery for a gastric carcinoma, for example). Therapy was arranged in the first session without further ado.

But for many situations it is not so easy. The principle is the same whatever the setting. The clinician must be seen to take the patient seriously at the somatic level, taking into consideration the patient's acculturation, expectations, misconceptions, presuppositions and status of trust in respect of the doctor. This is a crucial element in management. The moment some patients sense that the clinician is not taking his somatic aspects seriously, and that she may be pushing her into a psychological framework without respect for the body, then confidence will drain away.

Faced then with the patient at the end of history taking, examination, and whatever tests can be done at the time of the first assessment (skin testing, electrocardiogram, urine testing, endoscopy, pulmonary function tests, and so on), a management plan is set out which includes all tests and interventions aimed at thorough exploration of the somatic aspects. In my allergy practice, for example, this may include allergen reduction (such as house mite reduction measures), followed by elimination diets, and perhaps the use of some anti-allergic medication. The clinician in general practice or other types of specialist practice will deploy other somatically oriented interventions according to the type of presenting disorder. There is nothing novel in this, it is just good, ordinary, standard medical practice. The point is that such measures must never be neglected in one's enthusiasm for exploration of the psychological elements.

Patient Self-exploration:
Symptom Graphs and Mood/Stress Graphs

I want now to describe two very simple methods of patient self-observation and recording which can provide rich dividends. The first is the symptom graph. This grew out of my allergy practice where people can have many symptoms which I may want to relate to environmental conditions or diet, for example. Graphs are a lot easier for me to comprehend than a written diary, and I have come to realise that graphing can be of great value in many clinical situations far beyond the confines of allergy practice, to an extent that now-adays I will get nearly every patient to keep a symptom graph and a mood/stress graph.

A typical example of a symptom graph is given in Figure 5.1 overleaf. The patient's symptoms are defined and listed at the bottom lefthand corner of the graph paper, and the patient will record the severity of them, three times daily, according to the simple 'nil/mild/moderate/bad' scale. In these days of high technology I imagine that many physicians could not conceive of the power of this simple measure. But I cannot stress enough the usefulness of it, and I will explain why as we go along. But, at this point, several observations are pertinent. The symptom graph forces the patient to observe herself more objectively, and she starts the journey towards making connections between her symptoms and the events in her life, or other aspects of her functioning. Basically I am saying that most people need to be 'trained' to do this. The graph also produces a reasonably understandable record for the clinician to review with the patient at the next visit.

Another example of the use of the symptom graph on its own can be exemplified in the common clinical situation of the 'problem child'. The actual type of problem can be quite varied. For instance I use this approach with (a) behavioural problems, (b) hyperactivity or attention deficit syndrome, (c) any unexplained somatic symptom which may be due to somatisation, and (d) somatic symptoms of any cause where there appears to be psychological overlay. First, I define the behaviour or symptom(s) and list them on the symptom graph on the X axis. The parent is asked to monitor the severity of the behaviour or the symptom on the Y axis scale, three times a day. The parent is instructed to do all recordings without the child being aware

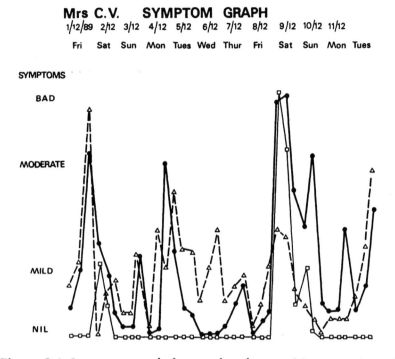

Figure 5.1 Symptom graph from a female, age 28, presenting with abdominal symptoms △ ------- △ , chronic tiredness ● —— ● , headaches ◻ —— ◻ and frequent mouth ulcers for 10 months following back surgery, preceded by marital breakup and back injury complicated by postoperative deep vein thrombosis. The failed recuperation led to further investigations and finally consideration of allergy. (Broom 1990)

it is being monitored. The child is never asked if it has symptoms as this would be too reinforcing. Furthermore the parent is instructed to under-respond to all behaviours or complaints of symptoms as much as is possible. The parent is in effect becoming an observer and nonreinforcer of the problem. The process of symptom graphing deviates the parent's energy into recording onto the paper rather than into the 'space' between the parent and child, thus tending to unravel the entangled dynamics between parent and child. Finally the parent is instructed to do something quite noninstinctive: whereas a parent will usually give the child much attention when it is symptomatic or exhibiting problem behaviours, and then relax back in relief when the child is 'good', leaving it alone, the parent is instructed to do the exact reverse. Thus the parent tries to minimise attention when the

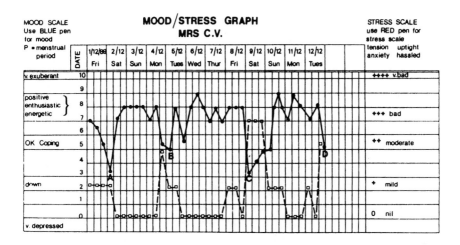

Figure 5.2 Mood/Stress graph from patient (see Figure 5.1). Note the stress levels ◦----◦ tend to be reciprocal to fluctuations in the mood (high or low) levels ●——● . It can be seen that the most prominent dips in mood (A, B, C, D) correlate well with symptom peaks (Figure 5.1). Recognition of these connections, removal of diagnostic uncertainty, and formal approaches to the question of allergy all enabled the patient to make a quick recovery without medication or psychotherapy. Put simply, the patient was suffering from an understandable, unrecognised, somatised depressive syndrome. (Broom 1990)

child is negatively presenting, but actually offers the child attention when it is happy and not demanding it. It is quite remarkable how often this sort of approach brings about profound improvement in behaviour and symptom reduction. It is of course a simple approach based on behavioural psychology but it exemplifies the power of simple tools and instructions.

I do not find that symptom recording on its own is so useful in adults mainly because it is the symptomatic adult who is presenting. I suspect that if family members were to respond to adult somatisers in the same way there would be equivalent extinction of symptoms, though perhaps only if the family doctor could be persuaded to under-respond as well!

Before I stress any other aspects of the symptom graph I want to introduce the mood/stress graph. The naming of this graph has some drawbacks but it is one that most but not all patients can grasp easily. Figure 5.2 provides a typical example. The way this graph is introduced is very important. Earlier in the interview the educational groundwork has been done and many patients will, by the time this graph is being introduced, be quite accepting of this task. Generally I suggest this graph after working through the symptom graph, and after providing appropriate prescriptions, laboratory forms or other therapeutic suggestions. This gives the patient the clear message that the clinician is not first and foremost, or exclusively, thinking that 'it's all in the mind'. I call this strategic tactfulness. I will have already pointed out to the patient that many conditions are multifactorial and that ignorance of the mood/stress factors might reduce the chances of controlling or curing the condition. This may sound like a warning, or even a threat, but it is something that most patients accept reasonably well. In my view it is in fact entirely truthful on my part. To defensive patients one can say: 'There may well be no relationship of your symptoms with mood and stress, but if we don't look we won't know, and if we don't know about something that is in fact there, then we won't be able to address it and we won't get a good result.' With gentleness, tact, patience and time, most patients will agree to fill in the graph.

Before describing how I explain the graph to patients I want to comment upon the chosen scales, mood and stress. The mood scale is an attempt at measuring mood in a high/low sense. The top of the scale might represent euphoria or mania; the bottom of the scale, deep despair and suicidal feelings. I assume that all of us are on the continuum between these two extremes. The stress scale is an attempt to measure anxiety. I tell the patient that it measures mood in the 'wound-up' sense, and I also offer the other synonyms of 'tension', 'uptight' and 'hassled'. Most patients will connect somewhere with one of these.

Both scales are in fact rough attempts at quantifying patient 'mood'. I know the terms I have chosen may not satisfy psychiatric taxonomists but my priority is to find ways of accessing useful patient data. If I must join the patient colloquially or idiomatically to do that, then, in my view, purist medical approaches, where essentially the patient has to join the doctor, are not appropriate. This approach certainly seems to work without introducing the patient to too many confusing (and doctor-satisfying) terms and concepts.

Even when explaining to the patient how to fill in the graph, I continue to educate. Remember that constant attention to education is a main form of 'holding' the patient. I start with the mood scale and using the point of a pen to guide the patient's eye I say that: 'All of us are on this scale, usually somewhere between "down" and "positive, enthusiastic, energetic'''. I am declaring that normality can include a wide variety of moods, thus giving permission to the patient who has widely varying moods to see herself as normal, or at least thoroughly human. By using the words 'we' and 'us' I am joining the patient on the scale, making it easier for her to accept herself at whatever levels she finds herself. I often say that most of us would like to be at level 7 or 8, all of the time, but that is unusual (at least in my patient population). I sometimes say that a few patients (usually men) come back having graphed a straight line at level 8, and that, commonly, these patients struggle to know what their mood states are.

The straight line may represent a variety of issues. It does seem that some people have such 'good' or rigid control over their moods that this straight line is a fair representation of their conscious emotional reality. In other people it represents extremely poor awareness of their own affective variance. In yet others it represents a defensive representation of their affective states; in other words it is what they would like to be like, or think they ought to be like. Most psychotherapists would regard any of these as a defensive and fundamental avoidance of unpleasant affective reality.

Before turning to the stress scale I ask the patient where she would have placed herself, on the mood scale, that morning when she woke up. This enables the clinician to determine whether the patient has really understood the task. It also ensures that the patient has got started, because some will have a defensive inertia and may end up failing to fill the graphs in. Further explanation may be needed at any point but some patients will remain mystified because they have very little awareness of high/low mood. These patients usually express mood in 'tension' terms and respond with more awareness to the stress scale to which I now turn.

The stress scale is on the righthand side of the graph paper so as to avoid confusion with the mood scale. But, of course, both are filled in from the lefthand side of the paper, a basic point which can elude the unintelligent, the anxious and the elderly who have no experience of graphing. The problem is usually solved by asking once again what the patient's stress, tension, 'wound-up' levels were when she woke up 'today' and marking it in with a red pen in the far lefthand column right next to the mood scale. In other words, get the patient started with her first recordings, so that she can see that both mood and stress recordings are made in the columns progressively from the left.

The fact that a patient may have difficulty grasping the concepts of mood and stress is often a sign of poor emotional awareness and a feature of the clinical presentation of somatising patients. The more difficult a patient finds it the more likely it is that such a process of trying to encourage the patient to develop such an awareness is needed for the patient to get well.

I also encourage women to mark down on the graphs when their menstrual periods occurred because premenstrually many women have a drop in mood and an increase in symptoms due to somatisation. Mentioning hormonal factors in this way helps to reinforce the notion that I truly acknowledge the somatic and biological factors in the patient's condition. Thus, subtly and yet quite honestly, I am again joining mind and body together, and within the graph we are integrating them together in a way that makes sense to the patient.

Having satisfied myself that the patient understands how to fill in the graphs, I will then arrange to review them and the results of other interventions and tests, in two or three weeks' time. I would warn readers that some patients will not tolerate just having the graphs to fill in without some accompanying somatically oriented tests and interventions. At this stage many will still be quite dubious about the mood/stress graph but will comply if there is sufficient honouring of the patient's somatic framework. Cutting corners is tempting but often results in disengagement. However hard I try, of course, I lose some patients and there is a significant number who do not turn up for the next appointment. I have worked hard to minimise this but it is unrealistic to expect to hold everybody. Somatisation is a matter of emotional defence. If the warded-off underlying emotional realities are so terrifying that any approach to them is potentially destabilising then we should expect a significant attrition rate.

The main reason the patient is asked to keep separate symptom and mood/stress graphs is simply that it helps the patient to keep the two aspects independently, which may seem odd when we are going to such efforts to induce integration. Careful perusal of Figures 5.1 and 5.2 will show that the X axes on the two graphs have different sized scales. Basically at this stage I am looking for clean data uncontaminated by any conscious or unconscious tendency the patient may have to 'fix' the data. My emphasis at this stage is the accumulation of good data, and helping the patient to self-observe, and beginning the process of self-observation in the two dimensions of mind and body. I do not particularly want her jumping to conclusions as to what the connections may or may not be. Nevertheless a few patients will make clear connections between the graphed symptoms and the mood/stress patterns of which she has become rapidly aware through charting. But the most common pattern is that the patient will chart them quite independently and will not have observed or even looked for any connections, until they are discovered by myself at the follow-up appointment.

The results of this very simple process can be very rewarding. Let us use Figures 5.1 and 5.2 to illustrate various outcomes. First, as in Figure 5.1, we may see that there are peaks of symptomatology. It does not take much scrutinising to see that these peaks correlate with the mood troughs A, B, C, D in Figure 5.2. It is also clear that as mood goes down, stress levels go up, reciprocally, and that is the usual pattern. If symptoms are so severe that they are always 'bad', then correlations of this sort can be less obvious. Sometimes this constantly 'bad' pattern correlates with a sustained low mood typical of a clinical depression. The patient in Figures 5.1 and 5.2 does not fit current psychiatric taxonomies for mood disorder but clearly her symptoms were mood related.

With a mood/symptom pattern like that shown above a patient may respond enthusiastically, full of gratitude that an answer may be in sight. Another will accept the reality of a correlation between symptoms and mood/stress but have no idea as to the implications. Another will accept the reality during the review interview but hours later will become highly threatened and want no more to do with it all, swinging off to a naturopath for a somatic answer. Another will accept the reality, go home, talk it over with relatives who erode the process with their own scepticism and resistance, leaving the patient caught in a very wobbly place between myself and these other powerful influences. It should be remembered that much somatisation is an expression of emotional realities arising in important and pathological relationships. Any challenge to this may not only frighten the presenting patient but also other participants in the system.

Sometimes patients will return with a straight line along level 7 or 8 and in this situation any physical symptoms will not be able to be related to the mood/stress graph. The pragmatic physician may shrug her shoulders and accept that there is no apparent connection. I tend to take the risk of telling the patient what I think about this sort of pattern (as described above), especially if I am convinced on other grounds that the patient is somatising. Some of these patients will reject this outright and we are left with any available symptom-relieving somatic remedies that might be appropriate to the condition. Some of the straight-line patients are so out of touch with their feelings, and compliant, and wanting to do the right thing that they will accept the suggestion of an exploratory psychotherapeutic process without anxiety. Some of these in turn will gradually start connecting with their feelings sufficiently to make very good progress. Others will remain very disconnected and have a poor prognosis. These patients fit none of the classical criteria for a 'good' psychotherapy client and require a skilled mind/body therapist if they are to do well.

Of course some patients come back with graphs in which I can see no correlation between mood/stress and symptoms. This is to be expected and in no way discourages me. Generally I have already made up my mind on other grounds that I am dealing with somatisation, and if the graphing supports this and convinces the patient so much the better. But mood and stress are very crude measures of emotional status. In fact they are derivatives of the 'real thing'. In my view the real components of affect are specific feelings like anger, rage, fear, powerlessness, hopelessness, loneliness, isolation, grief, and so on. These are often congealed into and experienced as low mood or floating anxiety. On the other hand the main expression of these more specific affective tones may be a somatic symptom. In these situations the mood/stress graph is not specific enough and will not pick them up.

The relatively simple process of graphing can be very remoralising and empowering for some patients who will come back quite delighted with what they have found. But usually the positive effects of graphing are more subtle. First, the patient has been very active in her own cause; she is doing the observing, and is being responsible for discovering the data and, ultimately, the connections. It is very empowering to be invited to join in the search for what is wrong. The usual doctor–patient relationship of activity/passivity is overturned, and the patient achieves a measure of control. In addition, even though some patients are anxious about what I might be saying about the illness they cannot help but absorb that I am interested in the whole of their person, not just the end-organ or symptom.

6 THE TRANSITION TO PSYCHOTHERAPY

What happens in psychotherapy? Is it just talking?

(Anonymous Client)

We have now reached the end of the initial work-up phase and have as much information as we are going to get to help us decide whether the patient is somatising. We have done the preparatory work in laying the basis for the suggestion to the patient that he now proceed on a psychotherapeutic approach to his symptoms. Having got to this point in my encounters with patients it would be uncommon for any to close the door completely on further interventions or involvement with myself even though there may still be a high degree of ambivalence, and I am still having to maintain a high degree of sensitivity and delicacy.

I now introduce the idea of psychotherapy to the patient. The majority have no idea what this means and once again education is needed. I will outline my usual approach to this in a somewhat stylised way. Clearly though, any explanation needs to be tailored to the particular client, and much of the material should be in response to the patient's questions and fears rather than in the form of a 'lecture', although this is the form in which I will present it now. What follows is an example of what I might say to patients:

'There are many different approaches to, and forms of, psychotherapy (PTx), and I want to make clear what I mean by it. In PTx you and the therapist meet together in confidential circumstances and in a relationship of trust, and you talk about the connections between your symptoms and your mood states and feelings. You may think that this will be very scary. In fact with a good therapist it is my experience that most people quickly find it to be a very good experience.

'We have had some difficulty sending people off to therapists who have little experience in working with patients at the level of

*the mind/body connections. In these circumstances the patients do
not do so well. To handle this we have developed a group of
therapists who are skilled in psychotherapy, and also do quite a lot
of work in the mind/body area. They all work under my supervision so that if there are any difficulties I can help them out. All
therapists have professional supervision as a quality control measure. You are entitled to know who the supervisor is and you can
be assured of complete confidentiality.*

*'You may ask how "just talking" will help. That is a very
reasonable question. In fact PTx is not "just talking". The focus
will be on what you actually feel from day to day and moment to
moment, and the relationship between these feelings and your
symptoms. This relationship sometimes turns out to be very simple
and at other times quite complicated and subtle.*

*'You will of course wonder how long it is going to take. The
answer is that I do not really know. PTx is not an event like
surgery. It is more like a journey. It takes as long as it takes and
that depends upon many factors, some of which relate to the
therapist and some of which relate to you. The first thing you need
to be sure about is that you can pull out at any time. The therapist may question that but it is always your decision as to whether
you proceed and continue. Second, I suggest that you contract to
do, say, six sessions for a start and then review with the therapist
as to whether it is worth continuing; both of you having the right
to question the process and its value. It is usually inadvisable to
keep asking that question during each of the first six sessions as it
usually takes a while to get going and to see some progress.*

*'Initially you may find the sessions very frustrating. If I am the
therapist I will normally focus entirely upon what is happening to
you as a person. Initially it may not be apparent to you that this is
relevant to your symptoms, and some people get irritated with me
because they may think I am not interested in their symptoms and
suffering. That is not true. I just know from experience that we
will make progress if we shift the focus, but if this does happen to
you it is really important that you express such feelings to me or
to the therapist involved.*

*'In the event you do continue beyond six sessions, and most
people do, then how long will it take? Well, world-wide, brief PTx
is somewhere between ten and forty sessions, and in our hands the
majority of people presenting like you manage to do the work
required within that period. It may seem a long time but, as I said
before, what we are doing is more like a journey; working through
feelings and feelings patterns is a gradual process rather than an*

event. The changes that occur need to be consolidated and if we try and achieve them too quickly we will end up with a poor result. But many patients make all the progress they want in, say, fifteen to twenty sessions; others with very different issues are content to take much longer, especially if the gains to be had are likely to be very substantial. But we really have to decide on these things as we go along.

'Another thing that is very important is what you can expect from a therapist. Doctors tend to act as experts and do things to you or tell you what to do. This is not what happens in PTx, or at least not in the same way. The therapist is of course an expert but she does not do things to you. Rather she is there to help you do what you need to do to get well. Some people find this frustrating for a start and some therapists do not explain the difference very well. The therapist will usually want you to start the session and sometimes this can be rather hard for someone working with the mind/body connections. If it is hard for you, make sure you tell the therapist. It is important to know that you are doing this therapy because you want to get at the connections between your feeling states and your symptoms. The more you discover your feelings, and label and express them in your therapy, the more helpful it will be to your overall progress. If you are dissatisfied with your progress in any way it is important to speak it out; in fact, in ways that you will discover, it will help your progress to do so. I think that is about all I need to say at the moment.'

Let me reiterate that this is my general approach which, in its full form, is probably only appropriate to the most intelligent, psychologically minded and resilient patients. Much of it is said in the context of dialogue, and much of it may need repeating in the first few PTx sessions. Remember: if you want to hold these patients you must educate them.

In the next chapter I want to look at a psychotherapeutic process with a somatising patient in considerable detail. But it should not be assumed that the path to PTx is chosen in a straightforward way. I will now outline some common patterns of proceeding:

1. Some patients who are psychologically minded and highly motivated enter PTx forthwith with minimal reluctance.

2. Some patients are partially convinced but still find it hard to believe that profoundly bothersome and somatic symptoms are originating in their emotional life, and enter PTx reluctantly or

sceptically, and it may take five or six delicately poised sessions before they are working well or engaged.

3. Some disengage and I never hear of them again; alternatively they wander around 'in the wilderness' for months, even a year or two, and then turn up again ready to proceed.

4. Some discover that in fact they are clinically depressed, opt for antidepressant medication, and refuse a PTx approach; some refuse antidepressants and opt for PTx; others opt for a trial of antidepressants and then, when they get a good response, develop motivation for PTx, being now more convinced that psychological factors are important.

5. Finally, in some patients with recalcitrant conditions where I cannot be reasonably sure (by my criteria) of the existence of somatisation, then I may spell out to the patient that PTx could be offered in a look-and-see way, in which both of us are taking a risk: I am risking wasting his time and resources, and the potential criticism of colleagues, especially my referral sources, and, of course, a personal sense of failure; and he is risking the waste of his resources. Being quite candid about the risks to both of us is usually greatly enhancing of trust and engagement.

7 PSYCHOTHERAPY WITH 'CHARLES'

Image-breaking is no less part and parcel of human life and history than image-making ... for the fixed image evokes the fixed stare, the fixed loyalty which may blind man's vision to the claims of further and wider loyalties, and so paralyse the human spirit and crush its inherent will to advance and venture.

(White 1952, p. 1)

Doctors and therapists working with somatisers must face the breaking of cherished inherited images or paradigms of disease and illness. We all find this very difficult. We also ask the patient to face the breaking of his images of his illness, and he too may find that very difficult. His psychotherapy journey will entail a further breaking of internal images – assumptions and judgements about himself, about significant others and about the world he experiences.

I will now describe a brief psychotherapy of such a patient. The course of the therapy will be spelt out in specific detail, using the material as a platform for a general commentary on psychotherapy with somatisers. The reader can assume that any principles outlined in previous chapters were also part of the process in this particular therapy. These principles will only be reiterated here where it is necessary to do so to give a clear sense of detail and flow in the therapeutic process, or where it is felt that the principle is so important it justifies repetition. Finally it should be stressed that this clinical example is one which was dealt with successfully in a brief psychotherapy mode.[1]

[1] It is assumed here that brief psychotherapy utilises somewhere between ten and forty sessions. In our hands perhaps 50 per cent of somatisers can be managed and enabled to become free of symptoms within this timeframe, and, speaking for myself, many of my clients will have a satisfactory result in less than twenty sessions. *continued overleaf*

1   *continued from previous page* There are a variety of factors which influence the rate of progress apart from the usual and widely accepted factors such as psychological-mindedness (many somatisers are far from psychologically minded until adequately educated), introspective capacity, personal curiosity, motivation, intelligence, language capacity, and so on. First, many somatisers are slow to engage and this process is greatly expedited if the therapist is skilful, able to tolerate the client scepticism, determined to keep focus on the mind/body connections despite client defensiveness, and is very sensitive to the various ways in which a client can be 'held' through the engagement period. Second, it is, in my experience, extremely difficult to ascertain at the beginning of therapy how complicated the therapy will be. A person who is apparently quite nonpsychologically minded may, with a little education, over five or six sessions become very hard-working and the therapy will be over in fifteen sessions (the following case illustrates this). Another client will enter therapy willingly and the somatisation defence turns out to be protection for a very fragile and vulnerable core: even a 'psychotic' core as described by Joyce McDougall (1989).

My present approach is to offer mind/body oriented psychotherapy to all patients I deem to be somatising because I am not at all confident that I can judge who will or will not do well. Indeed, in the approach enjoined here, whether the client does well or not depends to a large extent on the skill of the therapist, and the willingness of the latter to work in a situation usually regarded as inimical to the psychotherapeutic context, that is, with a client who does not know what the therapist is talking about, and who is highly sceptical as to mind/body connections, and whose motivation is largely that of having nowhere else to turn. This is not the salubrious situation preferred by therapists where the ideal client knows what he wants, wants the therapist to help him get it, and is highly motivated from the beginning. I respect Joyce McDougall's view (1989) in which, essentially, she warns therapists of dead-end therapies, psychotic breaks and worsening of the physical conditions for which therapy is offered. We have had scores of patients through our centre and these things have not been a significant problem, except that we have had our share of patients with severe somatisation, such as crippling headaches, who have required longer-term therapy (two or three years) for essentially the same reasons that nonsomatising clients require longer periods in therapy.

We certainly do find the occasional patient who will pull out of therapy before engagement has occurred, and some patients do get stuck in a dead-end therapy which has to be terminated, although we will try and reassess the situation and sometimes offer another therapist. The skill of the therapist is a crucial issue. Finally I would say that if we confined our attentions to the somatisers who were 'ready' for therapy in conventional psychotherapeutic terms, most of our somatisers would never get therapy. Thus I would challenge a common psychotherapy convention that sees therapy as a journey in which the main criterion for going on it is per-

Clinical Presentation

Charles,[2] was aged forty-two when first referred to me. Two years before he had injured his hip whilst working. Over the ten months before referral he had developed many physical symptoms including very severe recurrent chest pain, weakness of the limbs, faintness, difficulty with balance, neck stiffness and tenderness, abdominal pain, tinnitus, blurred vision, severe fatigue, anorexia, weight loss and rectal bleeding.[3] Affectively he had been preoccupied, socially withdrawn, irritable, and unable to cooperate in household tasks. His concentration and memory were diminished and he complained of 'sludgy' thinking, tension, fear and panic. He denied

---

sonal curiosity about oneself, and a conviction that 'this is the journey for me'. Some somatisers certainly fit this pattern, but most do not.

2 The client has read and given permission to utilise this material, and identifying data have been altered to ensure anonymity.

3 Somatisers present in many ways. Some present with one or two symptoms and others with many. Some present with alternating symptoms. For example, occasionally a patient will spontaneously report that: 'When my headache is bad my tummy pain isn't a problem, and then they seem to switch over.' This pattern of 'alternative' presentations is very common if one watches patient symptom profiles over time. The best explanation I have for this currently is that the affective energies expressed in somatisation have to be conduited in one direction or another, and sometimes they choose multiple conduits. It may be that one symptom expresses a microcomponent of the affective underlay better than another. For instance, fear seems often to be expressed abdominally, whereas control issues such as the 'containment' of anger seem to be at the root of many headaches ('my head is bursting with the pressure' of things that are not being expressed in verbal language). Inflammatory skin conditions like urticaria often seem to reflect rather more direct, but yet still somewhat indirect, expressions of anger or resentment. I do want to avoid simplistic hypothesising around what is obviously an extraordinarily complex process or set of processes worthy, I believe, of intensive research. But it seems clear, from my clinical experience, that different body systems at different times act as vehicles for different affective states and themes. A multisymptomatic case like that of Charles can be intimidating for doctors and therapists who somehow read the multiple symptomatology as meaning the problem must be 'organic' or 'somatic'. This is especially likely if the doctor has not picked up on the affective symptomatology, because so often the somatic symptoms are so distracting and worrisome that psychological enquiry is not pursued.

despondency or low mood. He had been given benzodiazepine tranquillisers, and a tricyclic antidepressant.[4]

[4] Many somatisers have some clinical features of depression but many also deny the subjective experience of low mood. I have come to realise that a poverty of subjective affective experience is a feature of somatisation. Alexithymia is the much talked about extreme form of this, although I have never seen it. There are nevertheless many patients who fit McDougall's category of 'operatory thinkers' (1989) who use rather intellectualised ways of thinking and speaking and who find it very difficult to pick up their own affective tonalities. With 'training' these patients do improve gradually with time. I often suggest to them that feelings (for them) are like wisps of mist in a forest of thoughts. The trunks of the trees (that is, the thoughts) dominate the scene, but we must focus continuously on the wisps. This focus on barely discernible feeling is a major technical element of working with somatisers. This has to be the dedicated stance of the therapist as the client cannot be expected to sustain this focus on his own. I realise that some therapists might be irritated by my insistence on the pursuit of feelings. After all, is this not what therapists do all the time? My experience is that therapists are not determined enough for somatising clients. If a patient walks into the room and does not know where to begin I will want to know what he is feeling. If I am five minutes late I want to know what he is feeling. I do not care initially what the feeling is about as long as it is a feeling. Training in picking up feelings is a major part of the early engagement process. I may actually irritate the patient as I pursue feelings, and that becomes a training opportunity as well. Too many therapists will fall back from such dogged pursuit of feelings and thereupon lose the main substrate of therapy. Moreover some therapists are only satisfied if the client will exhibit florid affective states and will effectively miss out on picking up on these clients' more subdued and subtle affective cues. Although the client's lack of affective capacities is in the end his own responsibility, it is the therapist's responsibility to be skilfully empathic. Empathy in this situation means developing the ability to pick up on minimal cues as much as on the ability of the client to develop his affective capacities, and as we all know these two go hand in hand. Many clients will improve quite dramatically, in terms of their physical symptoms, even though their ability to label and express feelings does not improve equally dramatically. Finally many patients have also been tried on antidepressants before they are referred to me, and most have not improved. Too often doctors see these drugs as some sort of sufficient test for, and therapy for, somatisation. Certainly they have their place but for many patients the drug is being used in the absence of other essentials: adequate education and 'holding', resolution of major affectively loaded conflicts, skilled psychotherapy, and all the other elements already referred to previously. Put these in place and previously ineffective antidepressants can be quite effective.

Charles was a short, handsome, fresh-faced man. He appeared tense and scanning, and walked into the office in a somewhat exaggeratedly bouncy way, sidling laterally through the door as if trying to squeeze past without being seen. I felt awkward and had to restrain an urge to reassure him. Though nervous, he was affable and conversational.

In initial assessment the first issue for me was to exclude serious organic illness. It was absolutely crucial to the future therapeutic relationship that I was personally confident that he did not have an undiagnosed underlying sinister organic illness.[5] I took out a careful history and performed a full physical examination. I assessed these in the context of available normal blood tests,

[5] The doctor must have the expertise (or utilise that of others) and in the end the courage to decide that no more 'somatic' investigation is needed. The psychotherapist must be supported by this sort of expertise. Again and again I see the process of psychotherapy (with a non-medical therapist) being undermined by the patient's doctor, who, losing confidence (often because of the anxiety of the patient), propels the patient into a further round of specialist visits or investigation.

At the time of writing I am struggling with a family who are greatly concerned about their fifteen-year-old son because of his hypersomnia (up to twenty hours per day) and loss of time from school. He has in fact been excessively tired from the age of two and there are features of cyclothymic mood disorder. A year before assessment he had suffered a head injury and over the subsequent months had developed many features of depression, muscle spasm, headaches (different from the transient post-traumatic headaches which did occur) and more marked problems with hypersomnia. There are quite obvious secondary gain elements and rather simplistic family attitudes to depression, medication and the possibility of psychological problems in youngsters. The point here is that they will not engage until a further clearance is given by a neurologist. Second, many investigations have been requested by myself partly because I want to reassure myself, and honour their somatic stance and their anxieties, putting them to rest gradually. But an abnormal liver function test has emerged which is hard to fit into the clinical story and may turn out to be irrelevant. It has stopped any further progress on the psychological side and has fuelled the family's determination that the problem is somatic. I think the boy is chronically depressed but I will have to bide my time, hold them through this tricky early phase, treat them sensitively so that they do not pull away reactively, and try and prevent other somatically oriented physicians colluding with them so much that the boy spends many months before he gets adequate therapy. Of course that presupposes I am right in my diagnosis. It is important I keep calm and unreactive, and to avoid being derailed whilst still open to any possibility.

normal electrocardiograms, normal radiological studies of the oesophagus and stomach, and reassuring assessments provided at the time of admission to a coronary care unit for severe chest pain. I felt sure that we were not dealing with an illness conventionally regarded as purely organic. But it was most important that Charles realised that I was taking his physical symptoms very seriously, as part of building up trust and engagement.[6]

The other major task of the first interview was to explore the psychosocial aspects sufficiently to ascertain reasons for the development of the putative somatisation, so as to gain enough detail to provide an interim logic for proceeding on to psychotherapy; a logic which had to be understandable to Charles. Thus the second major task of the interview was to construct a viable hypothesis that was close enough to the truth and sympathetic enough to Charles so as to enhance his sense of truth, but not so detailed and intimidating as to scare him off.[7]

So what did we uncover in the first interview? In the two years since injury had stopped him working he had been plagued

---

6   There are common problems here. If the patient feels I am not taking him seriously he may conclude that I am saying he is a 'hypochondriac', or that he is 'imagining' his symptoms, or that it's 'all in the mind'. This is so common a reaction that I 'strike pre-emptively' and actually articulate these fears for the patient thereby increasing a sense that he is understood, and giving myself further opportunity to explain my mind/body approach. I see very few patients with true hypochondriasis, and none with factitious disorders despite the prominence these get alongside somatisation disorder in the somatoform illness section of psychiatric taxonomies. Again 'education' is the key at this stage of the journey with the patient.

7   The most helpful elements in this process of developing a cohesive logic for proceeding to psychotherapy, in my experience, are: (1) skills and experience in psychodynamic formulation – most somatisation patterns seem accessible to understanding when one focuses upon covert affect and affectively loaded themes; (2) a developed 'ear' for the minimal cues provided in the immediate language of the interview; and (3) an initial focus around the period of first development of the symptoms. I am very interested in the events just prior to the onset of illness. Within these events will usually be found the connections (symbolic, parallel and reminiscent) of the patient's symptoms with the whole of his life and psychological structures. The seismological notion of a 'faultline' (borrowed from Michael Balint) has been helpful to me in this context. Readers will see an example of this in Charles' case history where the patient developed his symptoms in the accountant's

with uncertainty as to his future. He was also undergoing retraining from being a craftsman to an office worker, and he was
threatened by this complete change of direction and lifestyle. He
was beset by fears of potential failure, and daunted by his perception that his peers in the classes were 'bright twenty-year-
olds'. He felt badly about not 'providing for the family' and
abhorred his dependence upon government agencies, and his
working wife. I saw these as important emotional stresses but
they did not seem to contain sufficient in themselves to explain
the illness. They lacked the 'faultline' quality that I look for. So
often if I look hard enough I find a special piece of information
about something which acts as a vital trigger, or an aspect of the
story which is a key to understanding why the above stresses are
important, even crucial (but are not operative without the 'special
piece'). We needed to look a bit further. Like a detective I have
learned not to give up. Here, I did not know what I was looking
for but I knew it was there somewhere and that I would probably recognise it when I came across it.

We uncovered some more: there were important background
childhood fears of 'exposure'. He had always stayed at the back
of the school classroom and not wanted anyone in the class
behind him so as 'to avoid being vulnerable'.[8] He had an intense

office at a point where some fundamental terrors were activated. The idea
is that within the events just preceding the onset of illness one can, if one
'has the wit' (borrowing in this instance from Harry Stack Sullivan),
discern the essence of the meaning of the illness. One can reach down
through the faultline into the underlying affective reality. A peculiar or
unique set of circumstances (certain types of stress, symbolically important events, accumulations of factors which add together to set the processes in motion) arises in which the illness becomes an almost inevitable
outcome, a best way of expressing the essence of the matter. To achieve a
mind/body formulation in the first interview is highly possible in my
experience but the doctor must practise hard to become skilful at it. The
greatest impediment is that doctors do not believe in the mind/body
connections, and do not listen carefully to the nuances of the patient's
communication. Time and again I have insisted that supervisees go back
and look hard at the data already available to them; the result being that
the problem falls out comprehensibly before their eyes.

8 Was this going to be important material? The answer is, of course, that
everything is important, but this piece of information had floated to the
surface early in our encounter and in my view the material which
presented itself was important and had to be carefully considered.

continued overleaf

fear of speaking in public, or of being at the centre of attention. He had generally found it safer to be in one-on-one relationships and had avoided more complex situations. For this reason he had worked as a 'solo' craftsman. As I listened, this material seemed to have 'significance'.

His chest pain began suddenly on his first day in an office getting 'work experience' in his retraining programme. The situation was a large office with several clerks, in the midst of which he felt very 'exposed', 'vulnerable', and with no ability to escape. He felt he was being tested; would he fail in public? I immediately saw how the themes outlined above had primed him for this moment when it seemed that all the issues had congealed together to create a 'faultline'. Of course there were other compounding issues: much was resting on this first work experience in terms of becoming family provider again, and in justifying government funding of his retraining. His wife wanted him to settle and succeed.[9]

[8] *continued from previous page* Remember icebergs: that which presents on the surface is connected to much more beneath. Moreover this piece of information had, for me, a poignant and powerful quality and had the 'feel' to it that I was looking for: a piece of information which may capture the essence of the patient's affective themes. My approach at this point was to store it up and to watch for more evidence that it was important.

[9] At this point I was quite satisfied that I had enough interlinking data that we could tentatively formulate why this patient became unwell at that moment in the centre of the office. But why was it chest pain that developed rather than a headache or dizziness? I had not heard anything that I could interpret as a somatic metaphor. Perhaps I was not listening well enough, or perhaps I became so engrossed in the significance of the material involving his fear of exposure that I was not so focused on language or choice of words; or perhaps it was because I do not see many people with chest pain and therefore I am not so attuned to the somatic metaphors presenting as symptoms in the chest. I would be most interested to spend a few weeks in a cardiological clinic where I am sure that soon I would start to be attuned to the 'idiom' of the chest. Or perhaps there was no body metaphor involved in this case: the chest may have been acting merely as conduit for the affective energies for reasons that eluded us at that point.

Initial Formulation and Initial Management

My basic formulation was starting to emerge. I became convinced that I was dealing with a somatisation disorder. First, the fatigue, poor concentration and memory, difficulties in thinking and the panic episodes suggested low mood, if not florid clinical depression. Second, experience told me that all the associated somatic symptoms were highly compatible with a somatised depression or anxiety state. Third, I had gathered together the supporting evidence of a reasonably convincing and cohesive tapestry of underlying issues driving somatisation: the emotional predisposition, the precipitating accident and the psychological issues provoked by the change of career. Fourth, in the first interview I had perceived an inability to label and express powerful negative feelings clearly. I put all this together and concluded that I had a reasonably cohesive explanation as to why this syndrome had developed in Charles at this time.

I had therefore at this point established grounds for my confidence but of course Charles was in a different place. It was important to respect his continuing need to have the somatic aspects addressed, and to reassure him that he did not have an underlying and sinister disorder. The physical symptoms were being maintained partly by insufficient reassurance, and partly by relentless ongoing and unfruitful investigations, thus leaving him exposed to constant uncertainty which was anxiety-provoking and depressing.[10]

I then set up an interim therapeutic contract which had a number of elements. I was still quite tentative despite the fact that

---

[10] I have come to realise that a lot of symptomatology is actually maintained by the 'medical system'. The most florid example of this is 'facultative somatisation' (see Kleinman and Kleinman 1985) where the patient gears his symptom presentation to the clinician according to unconscious assumptions, which in this context means that the patient presents his somatic symptoms because he 'knows' that that is what the doctor knows about, wants to hear about, or will respond to. In this way, at least with somatisers, the doctor becomes a potent maintainer of the symptoms by rewarding their presentation. In a similar way symptoms are maintained by the negative ethos of uncertainty, anxiety and dissatisfaction which in turn feed into the underlying depression and from there into further somatisation – with a further cycle of medical help-seeking, a further round of investigations, or, in some cases, dismissive devaluation – and so the cycle continues. There is great therapeutic power in merely disrupting this cycle.

I was reasonably confident that the symptoms were due to somatisation. A too-dogmatic assertion of this was likely to provoke resentment and, moreover, my view was still a hypothesis yet to be confirmed by a satisfactory outcome in psychotherapy. Furthermore, in being tentative I allowed Charles to be tentative and to join the therapeutic process at his own rate.

Charles was in a difficult situation. He really had nowhere else to turn. He had explored medical resources at both general practice and specialist level, and had also consulted some alternative practitioners. I felt that it was important to intrigue him into a psychotherapeutic exploration of his symptoms, and also to enable him to feel that he would be taking such a course by choice. I suggested that we do four sessions together, and then assess progress, at which point he would be entirely free to decide to continue or not.[11]

I informed Charles quite directly about my therapeutic approach. I affirmed that I knew that the symptoms were frighteningly real. Nevertheless in the first four sessions we would studiously avoid focusing on the symptoms. I explained that this was not because they were unimportant or minor but because we wanted to get at the 'causes' underneath them. I said that it was possible that he might get rather irritated with me if he felt that

[11] Contracting is a difficult issue with somatisers. Personally I believe that it is impossible for clients to comprehend in any full way the implications of a therapeutic journey. I know that some therapists make a great play of the role of contracts in empowering clients, and implicit in this view is a rather naive view of a client's ability to comprehend. I favour therefore rather limited contracting. For example, a contract of four sessions was in fact congruent with being genuinely tentative and the low level of trust achieved thus far. The client's greatest safeguard is not a contract based on limited comprehension naively blown up into something more than it is but rather a scrupulous and respectful therapist who at every stage negotiates with the client in a way which is utterly respectful of his right to choose, and with a sensitivity both to his ability to comprehend and to his value system. All of this is rather highlighted in working with somatisers where we are essentially leading a person away from his 'chosen' way of seeing the world through a focus on the body and its symptomatology. But all therapy is value laden. This problem may be highlighted in work with somatisers but it cannot be escaped in any therapy. I find the best way to deal with this perennial problem is with frankness, respect, sensitivity and equal power, or, in short, by operating together in a thoroughly honourable and appropriate intimate relationship.

I was ignoring his suffering and pressing him for feelings, feelings, feelings. I said that quite often people feel like this and if he did so I would be pleased if he shared these feelings with me. In this way I was educating, pre-empting a problem which may have made the first four sessions unproductive, and encouraging him to feel that from the beginning any feelings and especially negative feelings would be welcome in the relationship.

In addition I asked him to fill in mood/stress and symptom graphs. I may not use the data accumulated but this request gives another clear signal as to the importance of feelings in relation to his symptoms, and he may start to find the discipline of making such observations helpful to him to make important mind/body connections.

I also suggested that he increase the dosage of the antidepressant on the supposition that we may be dealing with an inadequately treated depression, the reasoning being that if he improved dramatically on the increased dosage then this may well facilitate him in his move to a mind/body paradigm for his illness.[12]

At the end of the session I was tired but pleased with the progress thus far. Charles had come on the recommendation of his doctor rather than out of any conviction that I could help him; out of desperation rather than out of understanding, and

---

[12] Many psychotherapy traditions would frown on this mixing of psychotherapist and doctor roles, and there would be encouragement to delegate the prescribing to another at this point. There is a compelling case for this view and of course with the nonmedical therapist it is a necessity. I find that combining the two roles works in the client's favour, in that it allows him to experience in our immediate relationship my respect for his physical/biological functioning as well as his emotional functioning. We are, as it were, integrating him as we go along. Separating the two aspects tends to give a nonintegrative message. This way of splitting functions arises in part from our pervasively dualistic either/or Western cultural world view, though of course practicality demands specialisation because nobody can hope to be competent on all fronts. I like to combine the two roles but it is critical for me to watch that the 'journey together' approach of psychotherapy is not eroded by the 'treatment approach' so often characterising the medical 'active doctor–passive patient' model. Actually I practise the 'journey together' approach in my doctor role with highly satisfying results. In this way the question of prescribing becomes a cooperative 'process' between myself as therapist and the client and is as much an issue of therapy as anything else. *continued overleaf*

certainly not with a view to psychotherapy. I had to squeeze in a large number of what I found to be essential ingredients, to ensure engagement. The reality was that our agendas were incongruent, my agenda becoming affect-oriented and psychotherapeutic, and his agenda being a somatic emphasis and symptom relief. Of course we did share the more basic agenda of full resolution of the problems.

In addition, perhaps as a reflection of excessive responsibility taking, I found it stressful because I knew that if the session went badly then Charles would probably pull out of the process and enter another long phase of medical investigation, or just struggle along, crippled by his symptoms. There was also the tiring mental effort of finding fruitful and helpful language that would engage rather than estrange, and there was no place for 'formulae' in this task because clients are all so different in their presuppositions and language capacity.

But, finally, I think the most tiring aspect was my need to do this sort of work well. Charles, like so many patients, was highly sceptical as to mind/body connections, as are so many of the doctors who refer them. I was tempted to work too hard for fear of being discredited. In a culture where, conventionally, we actively compartmentalise mind and body, patients with mind/body disorders present a powerful provocation to tendencies within me, first, to break out of the medical status quo, and, second, the need to feel accepted by the medical community.

The Psychotherapeutic Strategy

At this point I had a clear and reasonably simple therapeutic strategy which included the following considerations:

12 *continued from previous page* Nevertheless it is important to be aware that a variety of transferences may be activated by the question of medication, for example: Am I as therapist being abstinent or gratifying in respect of this client's issues; or in what way am I colluding with active/passive issues? In my view the answer to these problems is not to avoid them by referring them to another doctor but to deal with them by ascertaining what issues are in fact activated by the prescribing, and inevitably these issues will be intimately connected with the client's important therapeutic issues. This all presupposes that the therapist is appropriately skilled, but if this is not so then it may be more expedient to split the roles.

1. The primary objective was to help Charles to develop awareness of the connection between symptoms and underlying affects. Experience told me that once he could own and begin actively to initiate work on these connections a conventional psychotherapeutic relationship would ensue.

2. Once Charles began working hard on affective themes it was likely that the physical symptoms would drop off.

3. One inescapable reality for Charles and myself was the fact that he and his third-party funder were primarily interested in symptom relief and a return to work. Thus I had in mind a brief therapy characterised by rigorous affect-orientation, but with conspicuous cognitive and educational elements, and with some emphasis on psychodynamics as a structure for understanding the meaning of conversion of troublesome affects into physical symptoms. I anticipated that perhaps twenty sessions would be needed.

The Therapy Sessions

I began the first session by asking him what he was feeling 'right now', so as to establish a pattern of 'insisting' that we face his immediate feelings, moment by moment. He declared himself to be 'pee'd off', frustrated with progress thus far,[13] disappointed in himself because he was frightened to go to the polytechnic institute

---

[13] Here was the first challenge to the therapist; in the first five minutes of therapy the client was already complaining about the slowness of progress! A great deal of patience is required in these situations because although the client may have given intellectual assent to the concept of a sustained and gradual journey, it often dawns on them only slowly that this is indeed the reality. Most therapists like to work with the enthusiastic and willing and although these do occur amongst the somatising population, they are a minority. In situations like this it is hard not to feel that the client is not taking sufficient responsibility, or that he is not suitable for therapy, or not ready. Gradually, however, this changes and the client can become his own protagonist. If one can keep in mind that the client is undergoing a conversion process from a somatic to a psychological orientation, and that it is the therapist's task to ease that process, then it becomes possible for the therapist to endure considerable difficulty in the form of scepticism, impatience, hostility and even devaluation of the therapist's skills.

where he was retraining, and stated he was a willing and honest person. He went on to complain vigorously about his physical symptoms: 'I still feel there is something wrong with my body.' He expressed grave doubt and scepticism as to the mind/body hypothesis, and intense fear that something was going to stop and 'I'm going to die'. For him the symptoms were 'so real'.

To try and steer him away from the physical symptoms, and to get access to underlying issues, I asked him if he minded if I took out a personal background history. Although I felt I needed this to establish a psychodynamic framework, I also felt that it could stir up affect-laden material with which we could 'practise' labelling and expressing negative feelings.

A number of important themes emerged. The first was that from early primary school he remembered feeling a terrifying 'lostness', 'all at sea', not knowing the school routine and never feeling 'part of the team' in sport, even though he was a very good sportsman, and indeed near the top of the class academically. So from early on he could remember feelings of not fitting in, not belonging, the need to protect himself by avoiding public exposure or responsibility for presentation in front of groups. I was encouraged by his ability to see the similarities between these feelings and some of the feelings he was having at the polytechnic, and in particular the fear surrounding his vulnerable position in the accountant's office. He could make such connections but understandably they did not remain in focus for long.

A second theme concerned the parental marital breakup occurring when he was thirteen. He became very tense as he talked about his father, with whom he could not recall any closeness. Eventually he was able to say how much he hated him because he 'did nothing with us'. He was a 'slob' who 'never contributed to the family', and 'made promises to do things for us but never fulfilled them'. Charles was resentful at having to become the 'man of the house'. There was a hint of sadness at what could have been and was not. Again, with some nudging, he was able to identify his own fears of not being a good provider, or a good father. Clearly the accident and its sequelae exposed this theme or 'faultline'.

His working career had involved many jobs including some university work and eventually the establishing of himself as a tradesman, providing well for his family, and surviving somewhat insulated from his underlying major themes by doing excellent work, avoiding social threat by working alone, and avoiding intellectual failure by staying in work below his intellectual potential. But the accident and injury, and being thrust into re-education, had brought all these issues into question again. Although the discussion in this session around these issues was not particularly deep, he was beginning to see that his experiences within his family of origin may well have set the stage in some way for his subsequent predicament.

Finally, there was revealed a strong historical pattern of somatisation. Between the ages of four and seven he had suffered from recurrent 'bad headaches'. During university studies he had 'sore necks', probably tension related. His mother had been very healthy but his father's 'sickliness' was certainly part of Charles' aversion towards him, making his own 'sickliness' even less tolerable.

I enjoyed this first session. He seemed relieved to share aspects of his story perhaps never shared before. I was relieved that he could make transient connections between the past and the present, with the glimmerings of a therapeutic alliance. I was also pleased that we had spent most of the session on the underlying themes and associated affects, rather than on the somatic symptoms.

At the end of the session I asked him to spend fifteen minutes per day trying to identify what his immediate feelings were during that time, and to write them down, particularly choosing a time when his tension or anxiety levels were high, if this was practicable.

At the beginning of the third session he announced that his physical symptoms escalated at times of high 'tension'. He was finding it very difficult to define the elements of this tension,[14] and constantly reverted to the easier task of describing the characteristics of his physical symptoms, and also describing his need for tranquillisers to relieve both the tension and the physical

---

[14] It is often helpful to educate about 'composite' feelings. For example, in this case I might state that 'tension' is a valid term but that it is derived from a whole group of much more specific feeling states such as fear, anger, frustration, guilt, dread, impatience, and so on. I might then encourage the person to stay with the tension and begin to label the shadowy specific feelings lying behind. At first this is usually very difficult and the client can only sustain the effort for a short period. Another approach is to say: 'I do not like words like "tension" or "hassled" or "uptight" or "moody" because, although they communicate in a general way, they do not indicate exactly what we are feeling – how about we struggle a bit together to find out what is inside these states when they occur?' If, for example, the client enters the session and is clearly tense, and can acknowledge that, then it is often a very helpful practice to work this out in specific affective detail before going any further.

symptoms, a point which he acknowledged supported the notion of a mind/body connectedness underpinning his symptomatology. I said how difficult it is for many of us to decipher the feelings inside 'tension', and I spent some time using diagrams on a white board, in an educative mode, describing how feelings can be converted into 'tension' or 'anxiety' or 'depression', or alternatively into physical symptoms, or of course both psychological and physical derivatives. I described how all human beings experience a constant stream of widely varying feelings, and tried to normalise his situation a little by asserting that many people are not able to keep in contact with all the raw feelings as they occur. A common mode of dealing with them then is to convert them into tension or physical symptoms.

I then suggested he choose a recent instance of increased symptomatology or tension and that we spend some time exploring the underlying emotions. He told me about his failure to go to the polytechnic the previous day but was initially unable to specify the feelings inside the tension which had led to this. But I persisted, gently nudging him to 'give himself plenty of time to get the feelings into focus', constantly bringing him back to the task of focusing the feelings, my consistent attitude being that although the feelings were not easily 'visible', they were indeed there (somewhere) and I would be happy to wait for them to become clear. Eventually he said that in not going to polytech he felt 'naughty' or guilty, and worried that he was going to put himself further behind. I did not try to interpret these feelings, but let them stand alone without embellishment, except to reflect on how good it was that with some hard work we could decipher them together, and that they were understandable and valid.

Another theme was his wife's impatience with his illness and her mystification in respect of what I was trying to achieve with him. I wondered whether it would be helpful for her to come in for a session with him. He seemed to tense up, and I encouraged him to give himself time to identify what he was feeling. At last with a struggle he eventually described 'apprehension' at the thought of his wife joining him in a session, and over the next ten minutes he discovered that this apprehension arose from his 'male image' and his 'pride' and 'ego'. He seemed to be saying that to bring his wife along raised questions about his strength, his masculinity and his ability to cope on his own. Again I just validated the feelings and stated that my desire to speak with his wife was purely to address any anxieties, scepticism and resistance in her that might sabotage the therapeutic process.[15]

In fact his wife did not come to the next session because one of the children was ill. But Charles came, saying that he now accepted that anxiety was the cause of his symptoms and that 'it is not a physical illness'. He was still dealing with episodes of anxiety by the use of tranquillisers, but he claimed that his chest pain has improved 90 per cent, the abdominal pain 60 per cent, and the tinnitus 50 per cent. His memory, thought processes, appetite and panics were also much improved, but, on the other hand, there was no change in his concentration ability or fatigue levels, and his neck ache seemed worse.

So by the end of the fourth session Charles was clearly committing himself to the psychotherapeutic process. For me it was as if we had launched our little boat into the breakers, and survived without capsizing, and were now starting to sail together on more predictable waters. I felt vindicated in my therapeutic strategy and elated at having survived the difficult part, and at the prospect of a really good result for Charles. This session was interesting because it covered many issues or subjects, almost as if we had to catch up with many present-day conflicts and problems to match his growing awareness of his feelings, and his growing awareness of the variety and multiplicity of feelings generated around the many little issues of daily life.

But the principal dilemma centred around not having *chosen* accounting, and a further frustration that in both his painting trade and in accountancy the work took him 'away from people'. He was a man of compassion, a listener, and empathic, and very frustrated with the restraints which he felt prevented him developing in this direction. He responded enthusiastically to the framing of these issues within the questions: 'Who am I?' and 'What do I want?'

---

[15] This is a common problem in work with somatisers. The partner is often left out of the difficult 'conversion' processes which have enabled the client to accept therapy, and will often erode the value of the early sessions with negative or sceptical comments. On the other hand many partners have been convinced all along that the problem is due to 'stress' and are grateful because the client has found a therapist or doctor who enables him to move down a path which the partner 'knew' all the time was the one that needed exploration. Sometimes, of course, marital issues maintain the tendency to somatisation and marital therapy is in order. Often enough the 'system' operates collusively in suppressing negative affect and both partners need to do work on their own feelings expression.

He was in a conflict of imagined obligations. He could not see himself being an accountant but felt obligated to the third-party funder of his rehabilitation. He wanted to finish the training because of the times in the past when he had failed to finish. Gradually he was able to identify his intense ambivalence within the tension states as he faced going to his classes: 'Will I go or won't I? If I go it won't be because I have chosen. What's more I might be exposed in public or I might not be able to keep up with the others. If I don't go I am letting the 'funder' down. I am not going anywhere. I'm not a provider. I'm a failure.'[16] We began to identify the uncertainty, confusion, fear, guilt and powerlessness, making clear connections between the powerfulness of the issues, the 'understandableness' of the intense emotions surrounding them, and the condensing of these emotions down into anxiety states and physical symptoms.

Thus far our explorations had largely centred around intrapsychic issues and in particular how he processed and managed negative feelings. But by the fifth session we started to look at the interpersonal aspects. This direction arose out of my nudging him to look at a recent 'tension state' and he chose an instance where his wife was critical of his mother. It became clear that he was

---

[16]   This is an excellent example of a composite conflict or set of conflicts or multifaceted intrapsychic pattern which, as a congealed unity, may get expressed as tension or as a somatic symptom or both. Obviously one has to be in touch with one's reality in a very clear way to have any hope of holding every aspect of it in focus, and it is hardly surprising that in the face of such emotional complexity many of us are unable to utilise the vehicle of verbal language and instead resort to somatic metaphors, many of which are rather like visual metaphors in their ability to carry, as an endpoint expression, the energies of these complex conflict structures. I now tend to the view that most diseases have such structures as part of the multifactorial basis for their pathogenesis. That will be seen by many as an extreme view. But as I go on I see many people carrying these complex intrapsychic structures usually unacknowledged (though acknowledged by all psychotherapists). I also see many patients with somatic presentations related to such structures; and I see them responding with relief of symptoms as the structures are verbalised and resolved. Finally, the scope of this approach seems to widen to include so many diseases that I have slowly – very slowly I might say – begun to see that these structures may underpin most, if not all, disease. In short I have been forced to become 'holistic' across the board rather than selectively or as it suits me.

angry with his wife but his way of handling the anger was to 'shut off' and withdraw, avoiding conflict and relationship disequilibrium.[17] I had a number of options but chose to remark on how unaccustomed he seemed to be, not only in experiencing his feelings in clear consciousness, but how labelling them and then expressing them into the relationships in which they were generated, in a direct and assertive way, was hardly an option either. To reinforce this I added that if at any point he had negative feelings about our relationship I would appreciate it if he expressed them there in the session. In the back of my mind was my awareness of his intense anger towards his father, and that some practice with expressing his feelings in a direct and safe way with myself and his wife could facilitate a later working through of this more fundamental anger. Thus throughout I was sustaining a constant permission-to-feel, feelings-validating, express-your-feelings approach.[18]

[17] I now regard many disease processes and exacerbations as reflections of what is happening in close or significant relationship. Again for many therapists this is stating the obvious as most of our conflicts and negative affects emerge within our relationships. But many therapists would not see physical symptoms as arising in this way. At the time of writing, I have just seen one patient who has recognised that his urticaria relates to unexpressed anger within his relationship with his wife and his quiescent rheumatoid arthritis was exacerbated within hours of discovering an old friend has Huntingdon's chorea, which discovery stirred up affects and conflicts connected to the death of his mother some years before. He is convinced (as am I) that his arthritis began in the crucible of conflicts surrounding her death.

[18] Notice my sustained two-pronged approach. First, as I keep on emphasising, there is the constant practising of feelings recognition and expression. This is the primary technical emphasis. It is so easy for a psychodynamically oriented therapist to become focused towards interpretation and then insidiously to lose this emphasis on feelings. If this happens there is a growing awareness that the therapy is becoming 'cognitive' and there is a growing sense in the therapist that he or she has lost his or her way, and a growing disconnection between what is being done in the therapy room and the physical symptoms. But, second, interpretation and clarification of the conflicts giving rise to the affective states, which form the first focus of the therapy, are indeed an important element of the therapy. As the therapy proceeds and as the client becomes more attuned and self-initiating with respect to his feelings, so the therapist's role becomes more to facilitate understanding and to provide an interpersonal milieu within which the client can track the connections between his emotional states and his physical symptoms.

I found the next two sessions quite difficult. Charles had become obviously more tense within the sessions, and much more reluctant to address his feeling states. I was disappointed, and irritated by this regression. I struggled with an inclination to be overly cognitive, in a 'lecturing' way, as if to force him back to look at his feelings. I was getting caught up in a sense of powerlessness and felt like I was reacting to surface elements. I forced myself to stand back and tried to catch hold of the affective undercurrents, and eventually it emerged that he was feeling disappointed, ashamed and angry with himself. The untangling of this flowed over into the next session. I sensed he was pulling back from his anger, and to do this he needed to doubt and devalue the therapeutic process. I realised that my irritation arose from my own self-doubt which was escalating as he disparaged therapy. I was actually starting to feel hopeless about the therapy. There may have been some projective identification operating as well as a stirring up of my own personal issues. He 'swayed' all over the place, deploring his inadequacy and lack of normality, and expressing hopelessness regarding the work we were doing together. With some effort I managed to remain calm and accepting of his fears and vigorous declamation, and managed to express hopefulness and gentle insistence on the importance of these feelings to his physical symptoms.[19]

In our next session he quickly began talking of how ashamed, disappointed and angry he was with himself, not living up to expectations, not being the perfect father or perfect provider. Soon he was talking of his dread of being seen to be like his father, a 'slob'; 'I wanted to kill him.' It seemed that he had moved from the defensive anger directed at himself to a more fundamental anger towards his father. In the eighth session he was extremely tense

19 Anyone working with somatisers is likely to experience this sort of episode in which both client and therapist struggle with doubt as to the validity of the process. Some of this is to be expected in a society where such therapy is hardly the norm. Some of it is due to unexpected dualistic residues within the client or therapist, such that when it all gets too hard, either or both fall back to previous presuppositions regarding mind/body separateness. Often enough of course the reason is more psychodynamic and transferential (and countertransferential). For example, in this case it may well have been that my relationship with Charles had got to the point where he was having to face within the therapy the hopelessness, anger and distancing that more properly belonged to his relationship with his father. The content of the next session shows this to be true.

and complained of intense frustration. After nudging he expressed anger towards me: 'It feels like I'm not getting value for money.' I was pleased he was able to express this anger (my pleasure developed, admittedly, after a few moments of disquiet on my part, as I wobbled on whether he was in fact getting value for money. I decided he was!). He also acknowledged his anger towards a defiant daughter. Recognising his anger with himself, with me, with his daughter, and with his father, he exclaimed: 'Good gracious, is this me?!'' I made some practical suggestions as to how he might work out this anger over the next week.

By the ninth session I was starting to get impatient with him. As I focused on this feeling I realised that we were stuck in a pattern in which my role had become the 'nudger': I nudged him to look at his tension episodes and discover the feelings underneath. But he had not yet developed an autonomous initiative and driveto be his own 'nudger'.[20] The process seemed based on my initiative rather than his. I explored this with him. Some things became clearer. His lack of curiosity had something to do with avoiding 'going public', a need to remain private. This seemed to relate to the shame he felt when his parents split up, and he remembered thinking of his father: 'He's a failure'; 'I can't take him out to show the world'; 'I can't say: "Here's my dad" '; and, interestingly, 'I started to hide my emotional life from my friends.' It seemed that showing his father and showing himself were deeply connected. In this way then, to ask him to be curious about himself, about his own private feelings, was in a sense to ask him to go public with his father.

I resolved to continue to raise questions about his feelings but I changed my approach. I asked him why he wasn't curious

---

[20] Most therapists recognise this as a problem in many therapies, and indeed some therapists regard such initiative and drive to be essential at the onset of therapy, and if it is absent the client will not be accepted into therapy. Most somatising clients do not have these capacities at the start of therapy and this is in part due to the fact that it takes some time before they are convinced of the relevance of the mind/body connections. With time many become more enquiring and successful with feelings, as did this client. In the long run the quality and the completeness of the therapy will parallel the extent to which the client can pursue his underlying feeling states with vigorous interest, can clarify them in clear consciousness and make good connections between the feelings and the symptoms they gave rise to.

about the feelings underlying an important tension state; or, did he think he had a reason for not looking at his feelings on this particular occasion? My aim was to get him to take responsibility for rummaging around until he was clear what was underneath his symptomatology. But when I looked at my own feelings a little more closely I became aware that my impatience with him was somewhat projective. I was actually disappointed in and angry with myself when and as I failed to look adequately at my own feelings underlying a headache or a stiff neck.

Another factor influencing his reluctance to pursue feelings was his dread of disappointment, seemingly related, in part, to his experience with his father: 'I won't let myself experience good feelings [in relation to father[because someone/something will come along and take them away.' Therefore to avoid dealing with feelings he resorted to somatic symptoms, or became critical of himself or myself (for example: 'Are we getting anywhere in this therapy?'). In the face of these tendencies I found it hard to sustain a calm hopeful attitude, a consistent feelings orientation, and a proper working-through of my own feelings of self-doubt, despondency and irritation as his symptoms or devaluations escalated. But despite my own 'wobbles' I remained sufficiently convinced that we were on the right track. I was grateful at this point for the clients I have worked with in the past with whom I have survived this difficult phase and gone on to excellent outcomes.

By the twelfth session he was reporting direct assertive emotional exchanges with his daughter and wife with rewarding results in conflict resolution. He had gone further and started visiting and talking with his father. He had resolved to spend short, manageable periods of time with his father, 'to get to know him a bit more', and he was finding his anger towards him abating somewhat. But whilst these themes of 'anger' and 'father' were being explored he was also struggling with issues of identity, purpose and meaning, aptitudes and choice.

Of great interest to me was his eventual clarification of the sequences leading to his attacks of pain. Feelings of lack of certainty, direction and purpose led to feelings of powerlessness, followed by a drop in mood and 'attacks of pain'. Previously an attack of pain, if left unexamined in relation to its antecedent affective processes, would seem to come 'out of the blue'. This then seemed like an arbitrary and unexpected attack on his 'whole idea of who I am' – an apparently random and vicious attack on his ability to handle life.[21]

Throughout this period in which he grappled with the issues of his capabilities, and the constraints on his options due to family responsibilities, and the question of obligation to the third-party funder of his retraining programme, he continued to work and rework through the relationship of his symptoms to his affective life, both in terms of the symptoms being secondary to affects and also giving rise to further erosive affects.[22]

By the fifteenth session it was clear that he was becoming more 'solid'. I felt his 'internal determination'. There was a sense of inner choice, rather than a feeling of constraint and of being moulded by external pressures, or perceived obligations. He was no longer tyrannised by a necessity to make choices immediately. He was attending classes comfortably, and his concentration and energy levels were much improved. He claimed to be 70–80 per cent better than on first presentation. By the sixteenth session he was stating categorically that he did not want to be an office worker, and was starting to feel fit enough to go back to his trade as a painter. This was for him a comforting possibility (in view of his family-provider role), but he also realised that being a solo tradesman was a somewhat self-protective limitation of his potential. Increasingly he felt that he was not obliged to continue his new commercial career despite the rehabilitative support he had received.

We discussed together how best to use the remaining four sessions available to us. He still had three months before the completion of his training course, and he needed to face the question of future employment. He suggested that we stop therapy and review the situation in two months' time.

[21] I have not put much emphasis on somatic metaphor in this case history. Nevertheless I do not think we are pushing the data too far to see his chest pain as representing the actualisation (symbolically and literally to some degree) of what he had always feared: that somewhere, sometime, he would be attacked, or exposed, and his inadequacy revealed. The work accident became then the precipitating event which led eventually to the second event in the office surrounded by potential observers of his assumed inadequacy, and all this congealed into the chest pain, which can be seen as a crystallised metaphor for all the issues, themes and feelings.

[22] The point I am making here is that any therapy aimed at resolving mind/body connections which give rise to symptoms will find itself focused on the ordinary day-to-day events and themes of life which, in these patients at least, are expressed in the mind/body axis in the form of symptoms.

I was delighted with his progress. He was confronting conflict situations by clear and appropriate expression of feelings, and subsequent negotiation, rather than by withdrawal and tension states. His relationship with his father was steadily improving, and he was committed to seeing him regularly, and being appropriately direct and assertive with him as well. He was attending classes, content that this time he was going to complete the course, and was able to reason clearly that even if he did not become an office worker, the skills and experience required might well enhance his chances in other employment choices. He was able to fend off imagined external expectations, seeing them as residues of maternal and private school pressures, and indeed a reaction to his father's failures. He was now able to stay comfortably in the classes without undue anxiety, although he still experienced some when the focus of the class was upon him. Nevertheless there was no longer escalation of this into panic or avoidance behaviour. He expressed hope for the future and this seemed based on a trust that when his course was over he could rely on an opening up of opportunities, and respond with healthy decisions.

We met again after two months. Progress had been sustained but we were both puzzled as to why he continued to get pain most days. It was severe, frightening, and at times interfering with his daily functioning. Occasionally it lasted for some hours. Despite understandable lapses he was 'faithfully' endeavouring to track the emotional antecedents to any episode of tension or physical symptomatology.

I wondered whether there was some as yet unrecognised factor perpetuating the pain response. As I looked back over his journey with me and at the pattern of his improvement I could not put aside the perception that he greatly improved when he chose to explore and take charge of his emotional life. Maybe this notion had some relevance to control of his pain? Having no idea as to what such a notion might mean for him I wondered aloud whether he could now choose to find a way to say 'no' to the pain or the expression thereof.[23] Was it possible that he had the power to stifle the expression of physical pain at its onset, rather than to allow it to continue almost autonomously as a habitual conditioned response? I expressed this in a rather tentative and wondering way, leaving him to infer, correctly, that I believed that he had within him the resources, the observational powers, the choosing ability and the efficacy to achieve such control.

I saw him again six and nine weeks later. It was fascinating to see that he was able to terminate his pain within two or three minutes of onset. He now saw his symptoms as a trivial but helpful reminder to look at what was happening to him emotionally. He was buoyant at having completed his diploma, and felt he had abated his sense of examination failure. He was considering a range of work options and seemed content to explore the various possibilities patiently. He was relieved that he was no longer receiving rehabilitative support, and he talked very realistically about various relationship issues.

We both agreed that the time to terminate had arrived. He expressed cautious optimism about the future. We reviewed the hard parts of our journey together. He recalled his intense scepticism as to my somatisation hypothesis, and I recalled my anxiety that somehow I would behave or speak so as to increase his scepticism and contribute to his disengagement. We laughed together about how different things were now. He expressed residual wonderings as to how such things could happen, but also gratitude for his new insights and capacities. I shared how much I enjoyed his honesty and sincere and humble directness, and my pleasure in seeing him so well physically and functioning so well emotionally.

I had a sense of exhilaration at having participated in his movement away from a narrowly defined somatisation and medicalisation of his internal issues, towards a much wider holistic view of himself as a person. His increasing conscious control over his pain intrigued me and left me wondering about the volitional aspects of the mind/body processes, and indeed raised questions for me regarding patient/client powerlessness induced by the mind/body dualism implicit in twentieth-century Western culture and pervading modern medical practice.

I spoke to Charles again after eighteen months had passed, and again four years later. He was in good health with only rare and very transient occurrences of pain. By then he was in a teaching position and enjoying his public role.

23 At the time this was very new territory for me both as a physician and as a therapist. My decision to intervene in this way was intuitive rather than logical and certainly not based on previous experience of saying 'no' to symptoms. The intervention grew out of the journey with the patient and seemed appropriate at that moment. Arbitrary use of such an intervention will, like any intervention not born in the crucible of the real patient–therapist relationship and journey, meet with the failure it deserves.

8 THE SCANDAL OF SOMATISATION

The basic starting point is the existence of particular, individual people and their varying capacities to accept or refuse a set of basic presuppositions within a historical field containing a number of options that one might define as dominant and recessive sets of presuppositions. What *is* a matter of history, however, is this field of varying options which confront the individual at any particular period of time. It will usually be the case that the dominant set of presuppositions will have such force and power that it will inevitably mold the thought and beliefs of by far the major part of the population within which that set of presuppositions exists. Minority beliefs, or individual thinkers who question the dominant set of presuppositions will then usually figure as incidental and unimportant eddies or crosscurrents within the broadly flowing central stream representing the dominant set of presuppositions. But it is usually well to bear in mind that changes or modifications in basic presuppositions are usually the result of the activity of such minority beliefs or the work of isolated thinkers who are prone to question the dominant themes of the epoch.

(Shalom 1985, p. 7)

Presuppositions are crucial. They determine how data are interpreted, and, even more fundamentally, they determine which data will be observed. Different presuppositions may lead to quite different data collection and different diagnoses. Kleinman and Kleinman (1985) have shown that when Chinese and American psychiatrists are exposed to the same group of patients the Chinese clinician tends to observe physical symptoms and diagnoses neurasthenia, and the American clinician tends to observe the psychological symptoms and diagnoses depression. On a wider scale, when presuppositions change, a scientific discipline can develop in totally unforeseen ways. Robert Ader (1995) has commented on this in relation to the burgeoning discipline of psychoneuroimmunology:

an appreciation of the integrated nature of adaptive functions unveils breathtaking glimpses of panoramas that are not even hinted at by any single component of the scene. Psychoneuroimmunology, if not the most conspicuous, is the most recent example of a scientific field that has developed and now prospers by exploring and tilling fertile territories secreted by the arbitrary and illusory boundaries of the biomedical sciences. Disciplinary boundaries, codified by bureaucracies, are historical fictions that restrict the imagination and the technologies that lend credence to Werner Heisenberg's assertion that 'What we observe is not nature itself, but nature exposed to our method of questioning'. (p. ix)

This problem of what it is that we agree (usually implicitly, collusively or by default) to look at together can profoundly affect doctor/therapist–patient transactions. The notion of facultative somatisation illustrates this problem. This term refers to the tendency of patients to present to the doctor the symptoms which are most likely to get a response. For instance, if a doctor is not psychologically minded she may pick up less evidence of psychological disturbance in her practice because her patients 'know' that it is the bodily or physical aspects of their illnesses which will be responded to; or, alternatively, over time she will develop a practice comprising patients who will tend to present only their physical selves to her.

At the time of writing I have seen a woman with a four-year history of recurrent bacterial infections in her nose. She has been treated on many occasions by two general practitioners and two specialists. Her condition began when she was doing a particularly difficult task for her company. She had been promised substantial rewards for successful completion. What had 'got up her nose' was that the work had been extremely onerous, delicate and personally costly, and the company had failed to recognise this adequately, nor in the end to reward her as originally promised. She recurrently presented the nasal infections to the doctors, but not the story of her continuing anger at the injustice. Yet when I attended to the latter she said: 'You are right, I knew this all along, what you are suggesting does not surprise me.'

There are many doctors and therapists who are sympathetic towards the 'concept' of holism but are, in reality, enmeshed in a very physicalist framework of both thinking and working. Many others are guarded, sceptical, and even suspicious of new ways of seeing medical realities. This is to be expected. Ader (1995) quotes Schopenhauer: 'All truth passes through three stages. First it is ridiculed. Second it is violently opposed. Third it is accepted as self-evident' (p. x). Sceptical colleagues typically respond to the sort of material presented in this book by demanding research evidence, and in some respects this demand can be seen as an unassailable and typically scientific way of distancing oneself from the hard questions facing us all in the holistic task. Research on our somatic aspects of functioning is obviously a much less daunting task than research on our psychological or spiritual functioning, and many clinicians, including the author, have been happily preoccupied with research activities confined to somatic and material aspects of reality. Such research must be done, but it must be extended to embrace aspects of the person beyond the physical. It is untenable to shelter behind the lack of adequate research in the mind/body area as a way of justifying the current somatically oriented ways of practising medicine.

Nevertheless it is very reasonable for physicalist colleagues to demand reasons why they ought to be looking in the mind/body area. The emphasis of this book is practical and clinical, and any persuasiveness lies in the fascinating connections seen between the patients' stories and their symptoms, rather than on a tightly argued holistic theory of the person. But there is evidence bearing on the prevalence of somatisation which should jolt the most dualistic and physicalist clinician.

The Prevalence of Somatisation and the Manchester Somatisation Study

How common are disorders which are best seen in mind/body or holistic terms? Can any disorder be excluded? How much attention should be devoted to the mind/body problem in medicine and psychotherapy? The impressive Manchester Somatisation Study, first reported in 1985 by Bridges and Goldberg (1985), provides a starting place for a response to these questions. The Study was a survey in fifteen family practices of acute and subacute somatisation. The patient population comprised 2500 consecutive attending people presenting with both new and chronic (or recurrent) conditions. There were nearly 500 patients with new illnesses, and these were assessed by a standard two-stage procedure (involving first the general practitioner and then a research psychiatrist, working entirely independently of one another), and diagnosed as having or not having a recognised psychiatric disorder according to DSM-III criteria. One third of the 500 turned out to have a psychiatric disorder but only 5 per cent had a pure psychiatric disorder in the sense of being entirely free of physical symptoms.

Of the 500 new presenting patients, 19 per cent were suffering from somatisation problems when diagnosed using very strict and conservative diagnostic criteria. I regard this figure of 19 per cent as an underestimate of the true incidence of somatisation. An examination of the specific criteria used in this study enables illustration of a number of interesting points.

Diagnostic Criteria and Prevalence

The first diagnostic criterion for somatisation was that of *consulting behaviour.* This criterion demands that the patient must be seeking medical help for somatic manifestations of psychiatric illness, and is not presenting with psychological symptoms. This is of course characteristic of many somatisers. The somatic face of the patient's reality is presented to the clinician. But it is not as clean as this in clinical practice. Clinicians working in psychotherapy, and who take the time to monitor physical symptomatology occurring alongside the psychological turmoil, soon perceive the extremely common concurrence of both psychological and physical presentations of the client's core distress. But if one's objective is to study somatisation defined as physical symptomatology as the *sole presentation* of core distress then this criterion is valid. Basically, in this criterion the choice is made to study patients who only present with physical symptoms. This is very arbitrary and in holistic terms makes no sense. Are patients who complain of being down in mood (but who do not reach psychiatric diagnosis status) and have headaches, somatising or not? In addition this criterion defines somatisation around the dimension of personhood the patient chooses or selects to complain about, in the clinical context she finds herself in at that time.

The second diagnostic criterion was that of *attribution.* The patients must consider that the somatic manifestations are caused primarily by a physical problem when they consult their doctors. It will become clear later in this book that shifting patients from this stance is a major task of good treatment. Nevertheless it is clear that some somatising patients will be excluded from a study based on this criterion. If the many patients presented in this book were processed through the Study *after* they had had sufficient therapy to realise the emotional connections to their illnesses, and *before* they had experienced relief of their physical symptoms, under this criterion they would not have been diagnosed as somatisers.

The third criterion was that of *psychiatric illness.* The patient must admit symptoms to a research psychiatrist which justify a psychiatric diagnosis using standard research criteria. This is a very dubious criterion. Many of the patients coming through an allergy clinic would not fulfil DSM-IV criteria for psychiatric illness, and yet are florid somatisers. In this criterion the study becomes victim to an overemphasis on the precise qualifications needed to enter a well recognised disease or illness category (and, of course, an overemphasis on taxonomic labelling). A person who is 'down' in mood may not justify a rigorous diagnosis of depression (using current taxonomic conventions) and may yet be somatising. Basically this criterion subordinates somatisation to a physical phenomenon secondary to a primary psychiatric diagnosis.

An analagous example of this problem comes from the author's clinical immunology experience. For years patients with systemic lupus erythematosus were diagnosed by strict criteria laid down by the American Rheumatism Association. These were very helpful diagnostically in the more florid cases, but useless for a significant group of patients who presented with some of the criteria but did not reach the threshold levels required by the Association. In this situation labelling is in part merely a servant to clinicians who want to communicate and do research on a homogeneous group of patients. To label and attend to well defined disorders in a prominent and very recognisable segment of an extended disease continuum should not blind clinicians to the many similar but perhaps less obvious (because they are outside current definitions) disorders outside this segment.

Therefore, although tying somatisation to categories of psychiatric illness (as is done in the Manchester Study) is understandable, as one way of getting at mind/body connections, the approach does have limitations. From a holistic point of view it must be better to see the person as a unity, within whom at times there may be a sufficiently intense 'disturbance' to lead to somatic or psychological 'symptoms', or indeed both. The patterns and severity of these symptoms may often, but not by any means always, satisfy our disease criteria and taxonomies. These latter are observer constructs and should not become 'entities' separable from the person as a whole. It is argued then that this criterion, psychiatric illness, skewed the Manchester Study towards minimising the frequency of somatisation by linking the detection of it to *florid* psychiatric diagnoses.

The fourth diagnostic criterion was the *response to intervention*. Here, in the opinion of the research psychiatrist, treatment of the psychiatric disorder would cause the somatic manifestations to disappear or to revert to the level they were at before the episode of the psychiatric disorder. This is an attempt to relate somatisation to current psychiatric therapies, and this author suspects there would have been little emphasis on the sort of therapy outlined in this book. Again, as with the third criterion, this criterion may well have led to an underdiagnosis of somatisation because it makes the diagnosis of somatisation dependent on whether the psychiatrist believes his or her treatment would be effective. Imagine our scorn if our car mechanics denied the reality of our engine breakdowns on the basis that they could not provide remedies. Nevertheless this criterion has some legitimacy in that it utilises a clinically helpful notion that, 'clearly this is somatisation because it responds to a psychiatric treatment'. There is useful confirmation of the diagnosis if the condition does respond to treatment. My confidence in my own approach to somatisation has grown over the years as we have applied psychotherapeutic approaches to many physical conditions and found they have worked. But if our treatment methods fail because they are inadequate, it does not follow necessarily that the patient is not somatising. Such a criterion will lead to an underestimation of the frequency of somatisation.

Whatever the reservations about the criteria applied, the data from the Manchester Study are indicating something very important in that one in five of all new illnesses, presenting at primary care level, can be regarded as being due to somatisation according to these conservative criteria. The stated reservations regarding the criteria would suggest the figure is higher, even much higher.

It may be that this figure of 19 per cent still does not seem too threatening to the way most of us practise medicine if we are talking only of 19 per cent of the 500 patients with *new* illnesses. Many patients seen in primary medical practice are not in this new category. There were 2000 patients left with more chronic illnesses not accounted for in the Manchester Study. These patients should not be left unmentioned.

One would imagine that if somatisation were very common in the new illness group then this may be true, even perhaps more true, of the chronic or recurrent patient attender group. There are numerous reviews that give access to this area and the reader can refer to these for further information (see, for example, Smith 1985, Lipowski 1986, Goldberg and Bridges 1988). It is sufficient to say that most of the studies put the frequency of somatisation in this chronic group at 30–40 per cent. For instance the most common presenting symptoms in 4000 consecutive new patients attending a general medical clinic (that is, a secondary care service, and most of these patients are not presenting with a new illness) in a Toronto teaching hospital were abdominal and chest pain, dyspnoea, headache, fatigue, cough, back pain, nervousness and dizziness. About 30 per cent of these symptoms were attributed to a psychiatric disturbance (Bain and Spaulding 1967). Most primary and secondary care clinicians would acknowledge the high frequency of such symptoms in recurrently attending patients in their practices, and by extrapolation from the literature at least one in three of such patients is somatising.

The problem of somatisation may be much larger than these figures suggest. For example, let it be assumed that the 'new' illness frequency of somatisation is not just 19 per cent (which is unduly conservative because of the conservative criteria applied by the Manchester Group) but nearer to 30 per cent, and that the frequency in chronic conditions is 40 per cent. Taking the Manchester Study population that would suggest there were 750 somatising patients amongst the 2500. That means that one in three patients coming through the doctor's door is somatising in some significant way. Furthermore this high figure is calculated using dualistic presuppositions, which are not subscribed to in this book. Holistic presuppositions are likely to drive the figures much higher. The 'real' somatic disorders (that is, those illnesses commonly seen as purely somatic, such as psoriasis, systemic lupus erythematosus and various infections), looked at holistically, may have very important emotional roots as well. These are not even considered in the above figures.

It is concluded that there is a vast clinical population of mind/body disorders, the occurrence of which may be a lot higher than just one in three presentations to doctors. The Manchester Study indicates that general practitioners only recognise half of the 19 per cent as somatisers. Our experience suggests not only that many are not recognised, but also that they certainly do not get appropriate treatments because few clinicians are equipped to deal with them.

In the end, though, it is sufficient to assert that the problem of somatisation is extremely common. It is not possible to say what the true level of somatisation is because none of us have sufficient tools, skills or opportunity to discern the influence of mind and other nonphysical factors in each and every case. But if doctors were discovered to be missing urinary infections to the level somatisation is missed, it would be regarded as a medical scandal. The financial cost to the community must be enormous as undiagnosed somatisers receive often-repeated, unnecessary and costly investigations and medications which do not lead to any satisfactory resolution of the problem.

9 THE PERSON

Biological psychiatry – presently the dominant force within the discipline of psychiatry – is dominated by a reductionistic ideology – this ideology goes far beyond a mere conceptual frame for the treatment of patients; it defines *somatic variables* as the prepotent factor in the etiology of 'abnormal' behaviour ... biological psychiatry is a product of its culture. Unless challenged, contemporary culture will progressively regard *homo sapiens* as *homo biologicus* – something on the order of a highly evolved, intricately wired, and socially verbose fruitfly.

(Pam 1995, p. 2; original emphases)

Anyone who has stood up in a small rowing boat knows something about imminent loss of balance. Imagine that you have three legs, and that each one is planted in separate and equally uncontrollable boats. In the past I have often felt that my attempts to integrate mind/body/spirit aspects of personhood have been like trying to tie together, into some stable unit, three territories which have an unaccountable tendency to separate and go off in totally disparate directions. But nowadays I feel much more that I have all three legs in one, albeit rather wobbly, boat.

In this chapter I want to develop, out of my work with somatisation, a logic for personhood which is beyond the rowing boat compartmentalisations of body, mind and spirit. At a certain point such an aim becomes pretentious. Changing metaphors, it is absurd to imagine that a pot can hold its potter in its hands. So it is probably absurd to imagine that thought, a product of our personhood, can encompass the totality of our personhood.

Somatisation and Personhood

What does somatisation really represent within the total economy of the person? In my clinical approach I generally move back from the presenting physical symptomatology towards an underlying 'story', and its associated problematic psychological dynamics. If the patient/ client can grapple with this emerging story and resolve enough of the problems then healing commonly follows. This general direction of flow of clinical focus from the physical to the psychological would appear to presuppose a psychological ideology (contrary to the biological ideology scathingly described by Pam in the quotation above), an ideology that asserts that the psychological is primary in somatic illness, and that all one needs to do is to move from the superficial physical manifestation to the underlying psychological meaning of the illness, and there is a good chance that healing will follow.

It is in fact true that many patients present to us stuck in a pattern of chronic physical symptoms, and that an effective way to shift this is to get them to work in the psychological dimension. But it does not follow that we must therefore subscribe to a view of disease as being primarily psychological, and that the mind therefore is fundamental.

A practical example will help to earth this issue. A child suffers troublesome skin infections. These, along with some not so notable respiratory infections, cause the consultant clinical immunologist to wonder about a subtle immune deficiency. The laboratory tools available to probe the immune system are becoming more sophisticated, so she may be able to define an apparent physical abnormality, and it is possible that, ultimately, she might discover a genetic basis to this, and that some sort of gene therapy might become available. The infections may cease. In that event cure will have been found through a sustained and hypertrophied biotechnical approach.

Why do I say hypertrophied? In the above scenario the biotechnical approach is overdeveloped and overemphasised in comparison with other important and related dimensions. What was disregarded in that approach was that the child was in a family where there was much discord. Father had threatened to leave home, in earshot of the child, on several occasions over the span of many months. The child eventually presents with his mother to the family doctor with vague abdominal pains, and occasional refusal to go to school. The skin and respiratory infections develop later. Following along this line the astute family doctor refers them through to a family therapist who sets to work with the parents in helping them to resolve relational issues. A relative peace ensues and the child's skin and respiratory infections settle by means of this socio-ecological intervention.

A third scenario reveals that this same child is doing drawings at school which manifest deep insecurities in relation to his parents. He has been found smearing faeces on the toilet walls, and has to be supervised during lunch hours because he can be violent with other children. The teacher knows of a play therapist who is skilled. This therapist enables the child to express its fear, guilt, and rage, and also to communicate these to mother and father who respond positively, take themselves off to a marital therapist, and the child's symptoms cease.

This example situates illness or disease in a multidimensional system which is disturbed, and, moreover, can be entered through a variety of doors. A clinician enters through a preferred door and some healing may take place. Unfortunately a clinician's preferred entry point may lead her to assume priority for her territory of interest, and to assume that any disturbance in other territories is secondary. But the fact that a biological, or sociological, or psychological intervention is effective does not necessarily mean that the one is primary and the others are secondary. This is linear, compartmentalistic thinking which we need to examine more closely.

Compartmentalisation, Linearity, Circularity and Concurrence

Which territory has priority? Is a person merely a biological or somatic entity, an exceedingly complex cluster of genetically determined biochemical mechanisms, from which all the other characteristically human behaviours and phenomena flow? Is biology primary, and indeed the ultimate human fundamental? This is a materialist or physico-materialist view of reality. Is the body 'first', the mind 'second' and society 'third'? (We have not even mentioned the 'environment'.) Could the order be very different? These questions about priority reflect dualistic and linear ways of looking at the connections between different aspects of personhood, ways which have not thus far proved helpful in solving that perennial conundrum commonly termed 'the mind/body problem'.[1] The questions also reflect a basic assumption of compartmentalisation which may be erroneous.

How compartmentalised are mind and body in personal and clinical experience? This question deserves searching analysis beyond the scope of this book, but the problem can be illustrated by an ancient story. The Old Testament tells of the prophet Nehemiah who is leading the Israelites in the rebuilding of the walls of Jerusalem, in

---

[1] Campbell (1984) states: 'the Mind–Body problem ... is ... one of the crucial problems of philosophy; the solution proposed has repercussions through the whole field of our metaphysical and moral opinions'.

the face of intense opposition from local non-Israelites led by Sanballat, Tobiah and Geshem. The latter try several ways of stopping the work, and in the end resort to spreading a false report that the Jews who are building the wall are plotting a revolt and setting up a new kingdom, intending by this to activate surrounding forces against the Jews. Nehemiah's reported response is: 'They were trying to frighten us, thinking, "Their hands will get too weak for the work, and it will not be completed." But I prayed, "Now strengthen my hands."' It is very unlikely that a modern educated Westerner would express himself in this manner. The language shows that, for Nehemiah, being frightened and physically weak are two faces of the same thing. This is emphasised when he prays for his hands to be strengthened. A modern religious Westerner would almost certainly go the psychological route and pray that his fear be reduced, or his courage be increased. Nehemiah somatises the issue (whilst clearly acknowledging the fear), but our modern Westerner would psychologise it (very often to such an extent that any real awareness of the relationship of the fear to the physical concomitant is lost). It is tempting for us to see Nehemiah's prayer as concrete and primitive, lacking understanding of the real psychological nature of his crisis. In fact it is quite clear that he knew he was frightened. He says: 'They were trying to frighten us ... .' He moves easily between his fear and his weakness.

Let us contrast this with the approach of Goldberg and Bridges (1988), the authors of the Manchester Somatisation Study, who have this to say about psychologisation and somatisation:

Indeed, 'psychologisation' appears to be the more recent phenomenon, and it still seems to be relatively rare in many parts of the world. To the extent that it occurs at all in developing countries, it tends to affect Westernised elites. Perhaps we should ask why people psychologise, instead of looking for explanations for somatisation. (p. 139)

And:

In ancient Buddhist scriptures psychologisation was regarded as the original, most primitive, response to stress. It was regarded as primitive and maladaptive because it is difficult or impossible to meditate, and psychic pain is beyond the reach of medicines. In this formulation somatisation is regarded as an adaptive achievement of mankind, lessening psychic pain and exchanging it for physical pains for which there have always been treatments. (pp. 139–40)

It is clear that Goldberg and Bridges are very aware of somatisation. They would have no problem with the notion of emotions being expressed in bodily language. But there is a difference between their approach and that of Nehemiah. In the case of Nehemiah there is an easy interchangeability between fear and physical weakness. He knows them both. There is a fluid connectedness, an interchangeability, a mirror-imaging of the two. But in Goldberg and Bridges' comments there is a much clearer either/or dilemma. In a typically Western fashion they immediately confront themselves with dualistic questions which must be resolved; questions which come naturally to all of us. Is the psychic pain (fear) prior to the physical pain (weakness)? Is somatisation a protective adaptation, a defence against psychic pain? I suspect Nehemiah would have no such problem. Fear or weakness: both are there; either will do.

Most of us working in the somatisation field would in fact accept a linear and (possibly) dualistic 'psychological problem leads to physical problem' formulation as valid, at least in some clinical situations. This acceptance sits nicely with conventional dualistic taxonomies of disease. In these medical taxonomies somatisation (physical disorders which are seen as primarily psychological) might be estimated at say 20 per cent of all illnesses, leaving the other 80 per cent of illnesses to be construed primarily as biological. In this framework some disorders are psychological and some (indeed most) are very definitely not. This dualistic system seems very tidy, but how well does it represent the truth? The example of the child with skin infections (and many other examples in this book) makes nonsense of this either/or approach.

The Person as a Multidimensional Unity

A person is a cohesive unity, and it is this unified wholeness which needs to be emphasised continually. Gestalt psychology asserts that: 'the whole, rather than being determined by its parts, determines the meaning of the parts' (Strupp and Blackwood 1980, p. 2238). This statement acknowledges both the parts and the whole. But how we talk about the parts in the context of the whole raises many issues. We can so easily end up with a collection of compartments which then have to be integrated. As an alternative we could perhaps see the human person as a physical/psychological/spiritual/social/ecological gestalt. Thus at any moment in time this complex unity could be seen as expressing itself, or potentially expressing itself, in all of these dimensions.

In an attempt to resolve a compartmentalising view we could perhaps say that there are multiple possibilities of connection or flow between various aspects of the person within the unity. This suggests connections between separate *bits* of the person, implying therefore a linear and causal connectedness between various compartments. There may be some usefulness in this conceptualisation. For example, if a child has fractured a leg and cannot compete in the school athletics competition then she may feel depressed. The linear cause–effect conceptualisation (fracture – that is, the physical – leads to depression – that is, the psychological) is one description of the observed situation. There may even be further unobserved linearities. Why *did* this child get a fracture just before the competition? But perhaps we assume linearity because we are conditioned towards this way of structuring the data we sample.

Recently, one of New Zealand's most notable athletes stated on television that her injuries were not the reason that she was failing in some international events. She acknowledged that her most recent injury, occurring two days before an event, arose out of her ambivalence towards her sport. In her view, her injuries were the somatic expression of her holistic response to her situation as an international athlete. She retired soon after to get on with the life she felt she had missed out on. Is it better to see the injury as a consequence of her emotional ambivalence (that is, in a linear sense, and therefore suggesting that the mind disturbance precedes the body disturbance), or as just the *physical* expression of her ambivalence which is very naturally expressed in the whole, and therefore in both mind and body?

Some of this might seem to be hair-splitting but clarity in such matters is crucial in any movement from dualism to holism. Essentially I am advocating a movement away from seeing a person as *bits*, and with one bit as more fundamental than another, towards seeing him or her as a multidimensional unity potentially expressive in all dimensions. But this book is about patients, clinical conditions and pathology. Can this approach be applied to pathology?

If we see the person as a unitary whole, we could, for example, conceptualise pathology in a general way as being some sort of - intense condition or disturbance, *in the whole*. We would then expect this 'disturbance' to be represented in the dimensions of personhood, albeit variably, and according to principles which have to do with how the whole is assembled. At least under some circumstances we might expect this disturbance to be manifested equally and concurrently in the somatic and psychological projections.

Let us build on the analogy of Nehemiah as a person and engaged as a whole. His wall-building enterprise is physical, sociological, psychological, spiritual and ecological. Whilst he is engaged in all these dimensions a threat arises. He is frightened, his hands weaken, he cannot work and his faith is challenged. In this instance we do not have to ask the question: 'Which occurred first, the somatic or psychological?' They can be construed easily as different and concurrent expressions of the same story of the whole.

My point here is that such conceptualisations apply not only to Nehemiah's weakness of the hands but also to chronic medical illnesses. Recently, a man told me that his longstanding ulcerative colitis had finally settled. Quite spontaneously he said he was sure that it was entirely an expression of his relationship with his mother, a difficult and manipulative woman, whom he had tried to placate and get close to for many years. He finally gave this up, his mother died, and he has had no symptoms since. He also noted that his mother had so affected one sibling that he became mentally ill. Another sibling managed to escape by leaving home and not returning to any close contact with mother, over several decades. Apparently she survived relatively unscathed. It is interesting that all this was assumed to be valid by this man, although he had no systematic interest in holism or somatisation. Drug therapy had been helpful but never curative. The cure seemed to come when mother was removed from the situation, and the son finally gave up a need to make healthy intimate connection with a mother who was incapable of responding. It is tempting, again in Western dualistic fashion, to try and work out the sequences. But it is clear that this was a system with many elements. Presumably the tendency to ulcerative colitis has physical determinants. Not everybody with such a story would get ulcerative colitis. The physical elements must be fundamental to his condition, but are they more fundamental than the other obvious elements? It is hard to see how anyone could ignore the fundamental significance of his relationship with his mother, or the fundamental significance of his unique and idiosyncratic emotional response to his mother. They are all crucial elements. We could surmise that a holistic response cognisant of and addressing these multiple elements might have spared this man many years of suffering.

So often, when I interview patients these days, I am able to pick up quickly on two sets of data.[2] Both the somatic data and

----

2   I acknowledge that picking up on two sets of data, whilst better than just one set, is inadequate, and ideally we would train ourselves to assemble sets which are descriptions from the vantage points of family and social systems, ecology, and spirit.

the psychological data are there to be recognised, if one has the 'eyes to see and the ears to hear'. In the case given in the previous chapter, the woman with the nasal infections (who felt unjustly treated, and this had 'got up her nose'), is a good example of a multidimensional expression of her problem, in that a reaction to injustice appears to be expressed concurrently in mind and body, in overt rage and in nasal infections. Is there any reason why the nasal problem should be seen as secondary to the psychological reaction to the injustice? Can physical illnesses be part of an immediate expression of the whole?

It is not suggested that an intense experience or disturbance in the person, and giving rise to what we call pathology, should always present in every possible dimension of personhood. It could present in just one of the projections. As we have seen, Goldberg and Bridges (1988) suggest that somatisation may be a way of conduiting pain away from the psychological expression because the pain is too unpleasant to be experienced in that dimension. Or a child may soon perceive that its distress will be responded to if offered in the physical dimension rather than in the psychological dimension, and vice versa. There is also room to imagine that at times a disturbance may be most appropriately expressed in one dimension, but also have some representation in other dimensions. For example, in an organism such as the human where there is a remarkable capacity for language and abstraction the most effective vehicle for resolution of a dilemma might be in thought and language. There may be a minimal manifestation in the body to accompany the language mode. A man expressing himself angrily may also be aware that he is shaking. The language option is not so developed in the human infant who might then resort to a physical activity like kicking or throwing, as well as crying. So expression may depend on both appropriateness and availability of a dimension of expression.

An abnormality in any aspect of our personhood may lead to consequences in other dimensions. For example, some disturbance of the biological substrate might lead to a psychological disturbance, giving rise to what appears to be a linear causal process from biological to psychological. It would seem likely that certain genetic variations may lead to biological influences with consequent psychological changes and outcomes which lead in turn to further effects upon the biological, and so on. This would be a somatopsychosomatic sequence.

On the other hand an intense experience or disturbance might originate in the psychological projection, and have its main expression in that dimension. For example, when two friends exchange warm expressions of affection they may act this out physically and embrace, but they may not. The dominant expression is verbal. But it can only superficially be regarded as purely psychological, because throughout the exchange brain processes, speech and a sense of bodily wellbeing (as a consequence of being loved) are involved. In contrast, clinical experience shows that an important psychological process may present with few clues in the psychological projection, but rather as a florid somatic disorder. There is room for extraordinary complexity. Having conceded that disturbance may appear to be confined to one dimension or another it may be that these apparent linearities and compartmentalisations are more a reflection of our observing capacities than truly reflective of fundamental reality.

Attempts to develop holism whilst remaining steadfastly dualistic are less than satisfying. For example, Brown quotes Grinker, who suggests that: 'mind and body are two foci of an identical process' (Brown 1988, p. 328). That is more or less what I am emphasising. But Brown goes on to quote Reiser, who argues that we should be thinking in terms of a sophisticated organismic psychobiological theory which is circular rather than linear; in terms of somatopsychosomatic sequences rather than simplistic linear psychosomatic or somatopsychic sequences.

These authors are trying to encompass the unity whilst retaining a fundamental dualism. In my view even the word 'circular' implies a point-to-point microlinearity. A circle is a line with its ends joined. I do not think they have achieved holism. They have to decide which comes first. The term somatopsychosomatic also implies a physico-materialist fundamentalism. Certainly I believe that a word such as somatopsychosomatic does at times represent a clinically useful conceptualisation but when, for example, we get into the problem of medical disorders which present as 'somatic metaphors', we uncover a conceptual complexity which seems to go beyond these notions of linearity made more holistic by adding a notion of circularity.

Which 'Bit' is Fundamental?

We do need to face the possibility that some dimension or other of our personhood is in fact prior, or ultimately more fundamental. This is clearly a dualist framework of thinking. It presupposes that categories of mind, body and spirit are not just artefacts of human thinking but real compartmentalisations with which we must wrestle to integrate. A biological fundamentalist could practise something that leans towards holistic medicine whilst still holding that eventually when the biological collapses (dies) then the rest, the psychological, the spiritual and the social, will also collapse. A spiritual fundamentalist could argue that when the spiritual is withdrawn then the other dimensions will collapse. Despite the ultimate disparity between these two positions both the biological and the spiritual fundamentalists could conceivably practise a functional and pragmatic semi-holism, which honours more than one (if not all) dimension, in the here and now until such collapse occurs. In fact, in the here and now, the practices of both might even look rather similar. Such similarity or dissimilarity will depend on how strongly each conceives and perceives the various dimensions as both actually present and expressed.

But in a very real sense all elements are fundamental. The physical is clearly fundamental; collapse of the physical causes life as we know it to cease. A dead person appears to have no physical, psychological, social or spiritual vitality, at least as far as our ordinary perceptual faculties are concerned. The physical is in this sense fundamental. However, it gets more complicated. A patient who is 'brain dead' can have a living body but is not alive as we know living. The physical brain is still alive in a vegetative sense (albeit very damaged) but fundamental psychological abilities to think, feel and relate are gone. The patient is not alive in the psychological sense. The psychological is indeed fundamental, and as fundamental as the physical.

More controversial in a secular and scientific age is the possibility that the spiritual is fundamental, and the associated question of what happens to the physical and the psychological when the spiritual is lost. Even if one is inclined to dismiss spirituality, it is evident that both mind and body are fundamental to personhood, even if we cannot yet decide which, if any, of these dimensions is ultimately prior to the others.

It follows from all this that it is very unlikely that we can legitimately look at disease and simply assume that the psychological and the spiritual are generally to be disregarded, as is the case in Western medicine in practice. I take it further and assert that our first position with an illness should be that it is likely that this physical illness is a representation in the physical dimension of a story which could be told in another dimension. This is perhaps most obviously seen in a simple somatic metaphor where a patient's mouth ulcers clearly reflect very accurately and aptly the patient's inability to express verbally painful affects of fear, guilt and rage.

A particular illness may then be construed as a sort of appropriate crystallisation, or focal precipitation, or the only available expression of what is happening to the person, within the person, between that person and other persons, and between that person and his physical environment, and between that person and the wider spriritual reality.

If this is true then it might be argued that the approach in this book is not consistent with such a model. The movement of therapy enjoined here has been from the physical symptoms back towards a 'story' which is seen as giving rise to the symptoms. I could be accused of being inconsistent, failing in practice to endorse a model that sees both dimensions as fundamental. There are several points relevant to this.

First, our medical and patient culture has hypertrophied the physical side to such an extent that patients never think to tell their story, even if it is clear to them. The story is nearly always ignored. The story aspect of medicine is atrophied and we can get much therapeutic mileage from encouraging the emergence of the story in the language dimension. Recently I talked to a man who had been off work for six months with an arm that was profoundly weak. He had seen his general practitioner, several specialists, and received acupuncture and physiotherapy. He was diagnosed as having occupational overuse syndrome. He received industrial compensation for the six months. When asked if anything important had happened just before the illness began he said he had wondered about that. Apparently he had been threatened with dismissal if he did not accept a new set of conditions. He refused, there was a stand-off, and at about this time the illness began, developing 'overnight'. The six months allowed a gradual working-out of an agreement. The point here is that the patient knew this part of the story but it never came into clinical consideration.

If we had a medical practice in which the physical and the psychological (and other dimensions) were attended to equally we would likely have no such sense that the psychological was prior, and we would be left only with a pragmatic decision as to which dimension we should expend our energies in to give the patient the best possible outcome.

Second, it is quite likely that the need to recover the patient's story is not so much a reflection of psychological fundamentalism or mentalism (or idealism), but of a more urgent need to rediscover the person as an 'I', as a subject, something that gets lost in the bricks and mortar of physicalism and biotechnology. As will be shown, this issue of the person as an 'I' is crucial, and an emphasis on the 'I' need not be seen as a return to idealism, whether in the form of mentalism or some sort of spiritual fundamentalism. The latter tends to shift primary causation, and priority, to some vague primary experience or primary substance, which is prior to mind and body, and which then projects into mind and body. This constitutes a move to dualism in another form.

The Problem of the Observer

Another problem which we must comment on before we proceed is the fact that we are highly constrained by our abilities to observe. We are highly conditioned by our inevitably limited and inadequate presuppositions. To develop new ways of seeing we need to loosen up these presuppositions.

In the woman with nasal infections we have a unitary being, a person experiencing injustice, a violation of her personhood. This experience, hers, is observed by myself, her clinician, manifesting as concurrent somatic (nasal infections) and psychological (rage) manifestations. Depending on the observer's presuppositional vantage point he might argue that this injustice is always experienced psychologically first. Concurrent expression in mind and body is ruled out mainly because of habitual dualistic, either/or, linear cause and effect presuppositions. At times this might be the best way to frame the problem. Certainly when I saw the patient she was expressing both the nasal infections and the rage concurrently.

When an infant is comfortably feeding on the breast and is then torn away, the reaction to the violation seems to an observer to be instant and holistic, psychological and physical. Of course one cannot be sure that the reactions are truly concurrent. My Western psychologising presuppositional system tends to conclude that the child became angry and then yelled, kicked and went red in the face. Nehemiah would probably see it differently: he would probably say 'My son is kicking mad!'

The frequent reality is that patients with illnesses present with the same story in both the somatic and the psychological projections concurrently. I am trying to emphasise (at the risk of being tedious) in all this that we are observing an integrated person who experiences, and who expresses him or herself constantly, and we observe that expression in one or another dimension, or all dimensions. And our observations are based on our presuppositions and are inevitably selective, and can create artefactual dualities, sequences, linearities, and even invisibilities (when we fail to observe). It may be that our tendency to structure reality into that which is first and that which is second is an inevitable consequence of our habitual and ordinary experience of time, a consideration which will be highlighted as we develop Shalom's notions of 'I-ness' later in this chapter.[3]

As a psychotherapist I am an advocate for the importance of the psychological both in personhood, and in its contribution to disease. Whilst I would see it as crucial, I would not see it as prior to other dimensions. I have already noted that nonphysicalist approaches to illness may appear to require a presupposition of a putative primary experience or substance which is itself dualistically antecedent to somatic and psychological expressions of the person, and in considering this question we come up against the various theoretical schools of psychotherapy, as well as the perennial questions of philosophy and spirituality.

Is the Psychological Fundamental?

In the last few decades neo-Freudian psychoanalysis, the object relations schools of psychotherapy, the interpersonal psychologies (for example that of Harry Stack Sullivan), and, more recently, self psychology, have all contributed very powerfully to our understanding of the complex processes of the significant relationships of infancy and childhood, and the part they play in the development of the person and personhood.

---

[3] Readers interested in considering how other concepts of time might lead to different interpretations of human experience, might begin by reading Paul Davies' recent book *About Time* (1995). Our ordinary experience teaches us that there is an 'arrow of time', that is, time has directionality from past to future. We are highly committed in our usual perceptions to giving priority in time to one event or another. Davies, an eminent physicist and acclaimed science writer, raises many questions about this from Relativity theory, astrophysics etc. Maybe it is time for us as physicians and psychotherapists to examine human experience in the light of some of these questions about time. Maybe our difficulties with dualism and cause–effect linearity are in part a failure to appreciate that (as in subatomic physics), with different eyes and abilities to perceive, apparently linear processes might look very different.

There is a growing interest in how these processes of relationship might contribute to the development of disease. The case of the man with prostatitis, in Chapter 2, is just one example of a florid medical disorder rooted in the vicissitudes of early development, particularly in the relationship with the mother, and emphasises the ways in which such early patterns of relating to the mother are repeated symbolically in later relationships. The relevance of early experience to adult experience is a 'given' for psychotherapists working in the psychodynamic tradition. The *story* I keep referring to, as another set of data alongside the physical manifestations of illness, is very much a tapestry formed from experience in both the distant and recent past as well as the present. The *story* is full of relationship issues. It follows that illness is full of relationship issues. In fact the more I look at presenting illnesses and disease, the more I can see them as representations of disturbance of relationship. This may not be the only way of seeing them but it certainly yields dividends to the therapist interested in the psychotherapy of somatisation.

Is Relationship Fundamental?

So we might favour a concept of illness and disease arising from a disturbance in the whole which is an expression of the person in relationship. In a sense this view defines persons as essentially persons in relationship. I have some sympathy with this view, but many doctors would react negatively, as their orientation and practice presupposes disease and illness to be a breakdown in the biological machine. The simple answer from holism is that all things are fundamental. There is no reason of course why a person disturbed in relationship should not collaterally have a breakdown in the machine. It should be stated more strongly. We should *expect* that a person disturbed in relationship will often develop disorder in the machine.

It would be a mistake, however, to see a conceptualisation of illness as an expression of the person in relationship as just another form of idealism, which in its widest sense is the view that the mind and/or spirit are more fundamental than the physical aspects of reality. To see a relationship-as-fundamental conceptualisation as a form of idealism implies that we assume that relationship is fundamentally immaterial, or rooted in mind/spirit, with the physical as secondary or derived. When one thinks of breast-feeding, or children at play, or adult sexuality, this is manifestly questionable. I think that relationship is best regarded as between persons as wholes, and having mind/body/spirit dimensions.

Any theoretical conceptualisation (from one of the theoretical schools of psychotherapy) of what can go wrong in the early relationships of infants with caregivers is of course a *psychological* description. Since Freud many elegant and helpful and often highly complex contributions have been made in this area. In a relationship-is-fundamental framework such psychological descriptions of early developmental mishaps are at risk of being invested with sole priority in the same manner that biologically oriented clinicians invest the biophysical elements of our functioning. Thus the psychological trauma will be seen as fundamental, prior and determinative, filling the stage, leaving little room for other emphases. But it is obvious that such reductionisms are as shallow as materialism.

For example, a lonely immigrant mother with a workaholic materialistic husband becomes depressed and increasingly emotionally unavailable to her toddler. The child becomes irritable, sleeps poorly, and his eczema flares. He looks pale and pushes his food away. How should we select from this data? What is the best formulation? The physician, the psychotherapist and the cleric will all select different elements of the story to respond to, and ask very different questions. Has the husband got his values wrong? What does belonging in a family and culture really mean? Is the mother suffering from despair in relationship, a form of object hopelessness? Is her brain biochemistry the problem? Is the child *just* allergic? Is the child starting to carry the mother's depression? Is the child suffering an abandonment depression? There are in fact many selective descriptions of what has gone wrong, but there is only one story, a multidimensional cohesive story. It is manifestly obvious that all the elements are important, all the questions are relevant, all dimensions are fundamental, and that anyone who wants to go the purely physical or psychological or spiritual way is clearly wearing blinkers.

Is the Unconscious Fundamental?

A psychotherapist wearing psychoanalytically tinted spectacles might postulate the 'unconscious' as fundamental in the somatisation drama. Thus the patient with prostatitis (Chapter 2) could be seen as expressing unconscious fears, in respect of his relationship with his mother, in the form of prostate inflammation. I am sure this was true. Those fears were there and his prostatitis was an expression of the same relational issues in the somatic dimension. To infer from this that the unconscious was prior in all this would be to take up a dualistic position with idealist overtones, a position which in this instance says that conflict in the mind is primary, and is then transformed dualistically into bodily form; that is, it construes the unconscious as prior to the physical, and determinative of physical reality. Again there may be occasions when that is a practically useful conceptualisation, and certainly the case of prostatitis could be tidily conceptualised like this.

Interestingly, the presuppositions of the notion of the unconscious were physico-materialist rather than idealist. The origin of the concept of the unconscious as a territory of the psyche belongs mainly to Freud. Shalom (1985) has written a fascinating and rigorous analysis of the role the mind/body problem played in Freud's development of psychoanalytic theory. He cogently argues that Freud was a physico-materialist who struggled during the 1890s, in the unpublished *Project*, to root mind processes firmly in bodily processes. In particular he struggled with the difficulty of explaining repression in neurophysical terms. The detail does not matter, and interested readers can resort to Shalom for an in-depth journey through this material. But what is interesting is that Freud appeared to give up the overt struggle, as represented in the *Project*, to integrate mind into brain (though again Shalom argues that the mind/body issue remained an underlying theme in all of Freud's work). In reaction Freud turned to a psychological focus, and psychoanalysis was born. Interestingly the terminology of Freudian psychoanalysis is characterised by mechanisms, compartments, forces and psychic structures, and Shalom argues that the Freudian psychic structures are proffered in this way because he 'molded *psychical* processes on the model of neurological processes' (1985, p. 171; emphasis added). The theory of psychic process reflected Freud's previous preoccupation with the neurological processes. He turned to a psychological theory, a theory of psychic processes, mirroring in its structure the mechanisms of the physical, and, curiously, the unconscious became, for Freud, the psychic structure that was rooted in the biophysical: 'As Freud himself pointed out in the *Outline of Psychoanalysis*, the specific hallmark of psychoanalysis is the doctrine of *the unconscious* as the *direct expression* of neural processes' (Shalom 1985, p. 169; original emphasis). Freud's position is fundamentally materialistic (the unconscious is seen as rooted in prior biological processes), and parallelistic (psychic processes and bodily processes are seen as existing in parallel), which is therefore dualistic.

This may seem a little academic but there are some very important issues here. How should we construe somatisation in a psychoanalytic framework? Is the sequence of disease development as follows: brain processes – abnormal brain processes – disturbed unconscious – disturbed psychic processes – defensive manoevres including somatisation – disease? This is of course offensively simplistic, mechanistic, reductionist, linear, and probably not representative of many neo-psychoanalytic thinkers.

However, I have other problems with an undue emphasis on the role of the unconscious in the development of illness. I think illness needs to be construed more often in sociological, relational and interpersonal terms. The focus of classical psychoanalysis firmly places the problem in the individual, and within his or her intrapsychic structure. There is this dimension of course. Disease then becomes, ultimately, an individual affair, downgrading the role of relationship (though of course it is recognised that intrapsychic structure arises or develops within relationship). It becomes a matter of emphasis. My preference would be to see many of the psychoanalytic emphases as valid, and yet to see the problem experience (ultimately manifesting as illness) as emerging in relationship (with mother, other persons, and the environment), and having unconscious elements, rather than taking the further step of making the unconscious an entity, and then giving it primacy, thus moving to a dualistic and idealistic position (or conversely, in Freud's original analysis, to a materialist position).

It seems that mind, body, relationship, environment and spirit are all crucial, but the difficulty is in how to talk about them in a way which is holistic, and which takes us away from 'the mind/body problem'. In an attempt to do this I want now to explore the issue of personal identity, the notion of the human subject as an 'I'.

Personal Identity is Fundamental

I entered the mind/body conceptualisation 'jungle' by the route of clinical practice whilst wearing the hats of both physician and psychotherapist, but soon realised that certain types of clinical presentation nourished a belief in me that some illnesses were purely physical.

'Hayfever' is in many cases caused by seasonal exposure to grass pollens, in a person who is genetically predisposed to over-react immunologically to the grass pollen stimulus. The medical profession can manage the symptoms pharmacologically. We have then a genetic tendency, a precipitating cause, and a way of treating it. Seen this way, it is a nicely closed system which appears not to need any extra dimension. In fact virtually no one considers the possibility that other dimensions of personhood may play important roles in the pathogenesis of 'hayfever'. We encourage one another to see this purely physically; any possible collateral 'story' is excluded. This illness *is* physical: there is no question about it.

On the other hand, a muscle tension headache will commonly be construed as emotion-related and classed as psychosomatic, or nonorganic. In this instance the mind is seen as influencing the body. This would not even be considered in the hayfever example. Thus in medicine we continue to appraise all physical conditions in a dualistic manner, and as long as we continue to exclude other person dimensions from conditions like hayfever we appear to be justified in this approach.

The problem I faced was that increasingly in the supposedly purely physical illnesses, I was discerning clear collateral 'stories' of apparently substantial significance to the predisposition, precipitation and perpetuation of the illness. What should I do with this awareness? Once I had established the presence of a substantial organic process it made pragmatic sense to treat the condition with whatever physical means there were available, but I was still left with the 'story', and how to integrate it into my understanding of the illness.

Gradually I began to conclude that we needed a paradigm or conceptualisation in which there was something prior to the concepts of mind and body, in which both were derivative. Eventually I stumbled across Shalom's philosophical work on the notion of personal identity as more fundamental than either mind or body. This excited me because he was providing a rigorously argued conceptualisation which was very congruent with my own intuitions which had developed in the crucible of clinical experience without the benefit of philosophical training. I will now try and summarise Shalom's thesis, which he developed in the context of careful analyses of the work of Wittgenstein, Feigl, Strawson, Smart, Armstrong, Place, Wiener, Sayre, Parfit, Nagel, Freud, Jaynes and Sperry (and many others in less detail).

Shalom argues that the person is not reducible to a *combination* of body and mind, and therefore the problem of mind/body integration is not soluble by working to relate mind and body categories as if they are the fundamentals. Certainly the failure of both philosophy and medicine so far to solve the mind/body problem could be interpreted as confirming this. He sees the 'existing person', or 'subject', or the 'I', as the ultimate: 'underlying the presuppositions of scientific reductionism there is a spontaneous and quite irreducible "subject" who does not allow even the declared reductionist to identify his internal subjective structure with his external spatial structure' (Shalom 1985, p. 407).

You and I have bodies, minds, souls, spirits, consciousness, and an unconscious. They are categories which describe important elements of our experience. All have at various times been given priority and declared fundamental. They are real but none of them describe who 'I' am. I *have* them. The 'I' is there, not beyond body, mind, soul, and so on, but embracing them. Something that *has* something must be prior to that which it *has*. If we get rid of the *has*, and define the person as a mind or as a body or as a spirit or as a consciousness, we end up with reductionisms which do not satisfy our whole experience of reality, and by many criteria do not stand up to logical analysis. So the 'subject' or personal identity, the subject as 'I', is postulated as fundamental: 'I am in effect saying ... that the body/mind dualism considered as ultimate creates a false dilemma in which I (the "I" which is trying to grasp its own situation) find myself trapped by virtue of the inadequacy of the conceptual framework used' (Shalom 1985, p. 411).

If then we situate personhood in a body/mind dualistic framework we will struggle forever, because it cannot contain what we experience as persons.

> If I put to myself the question: 'What or who am I?', my difficulty in answering stems from the fact that I know myself as both 'bodily' and 'conscious', and that I have an extreme difficulty in relating myself to what I mean by these two terms. And so I concentrate on these terms and thereby suppose that the *problem* can be expressed by saying that it is a problem of 'the relationship between body and mind'. (Shalom 1985, p. 411; original emphasis)

We succumb to the view that we must solve the problem of personhood between body and mind because these are prominent categories in our experience, and we then project the problem of personhood onto these categories.

Since my experience of the external world teaches me that relationships have *relata,* I tend to assume that the present problem can be conceived in the same way, and that the *relata* concerned must naturally be precisely what are referred to as 'body' and 'mind'. But it is just exactly in that assumption that I have made my fundamental mistake. To borrow an expression from Wittgenstein: the conjuring trick has already occurred. For what I have failed to recognise is that in the very act of setting out the problem in this way, it is I the subject, who am formulating it in these terms, and this has implications of its own. The implications are that when I, the subject, formulate the problem in this way, I have projected myself into the referents of the terms which I have used in that *formulation* – and I mistakenly assume that I, who am doing this, am absorbed within the framework of those referents themselves. ...

'I', the subject, experience mind and body but it is a mistake to absorb myself into a restricted system made up of these two categories. ...

I assume that the compound of 'body' and 'mind' constitutes an adequate substitute for the 'I' that is performing *both* the projecting into the referents of these words, *and* the compounding of them into the *theoretical* entity which I, the same I, now call 'body and mind'. But this assumption is simply inaccurate, for there is no compound of 'body and mind' which is not thought so by an 'I' which continues to think so. And therefore the compound called 'body and mind' can only itself exist as a theoretical derivation of the continued intellectual activity of that 'I' which does not merely think itself as 'I' but which constantly expresses itself as 'I', thereby indicating in act its own priority relatively to the construct 'body and mind'. ...

the problem is not 'the body/mind problem', but the problem of the person or the 'I'. (Shalom 1985, p. 412; original emphases)

Thus Shalom summarises the view that I had come to, that each day in my office I was dealing with whole persons, personal identities, 'I' after 'I', who, because their realities can be conceptualised and abstracted into categories covered by terms such as 'body' and 'mind', provide me with two sets of data which can be clustered together; in one case in terms of physical disease, and in the other in terms of 'story'. But they remain merely as focused-upon dimensions or derivatives of the reality of the prior 'I'.

A reader may well ask, 'What difference does all this make?'

Clinically it makes a huge difference. If I now look across to my psychotherapy client and she is battling with object hopelessness, and at the same time she and her doctor are battling with asthma, or rheumatoid arthritis, or irritable bowel syndrome, I do not have a sense that we have two rowing boats in a heaving sea, that somehow we have to tie them together, but rather that we have one boat – and I and the doctor are trying to get onto it from different sides.

The question then is, what is this 'I'? Along with Shalom I would say that the 'I' is not an extra entity added to mind, body, soul or spirit, but involves, embraces and subtends both matter and mind: 'the fundamental reality of "I am" is that I am "an existent" that exists *as* body and that exists *as* mind, and that this implies neither a third reality nor the interpretation of "I am" as body or as mind nor as an uneasy combination of both' (Shalom 1985, p. 420; original emphases).

This notion of 'existing' is important. 'I' am a sort of permanent existing. I remember myself going to school at five years of age. I know that boy to be the same person that I am now. I acknowledge all the changes in my body and my mind, which have occurred over the years, but there is something constant or permanent which is 'me'. Ask an eighty-five-year-old – is she the same person she was at the age of ten? At one level or pole she will say yes, and at another pole she will say no. Shalom calls these the pole of change and the pole of permanence.

Shalom is clear that this permanent existing, this personal identity, the 'I', underpins and expresses itself in 'how things are' in the modes we call body and mind. There is a distinction between the continuous process of 'how things are' in the modes of expression called body and mind (the arenas of investigation for scientists and psychologists) and something within all that is referred to as 'permanent existing' (Shalom 1985, p. 426). This is not dualistic. The 'permanent existing' is not a third reality separate in some way from mind and body. 'I', in my fundamental existing, am coextensive with my physical functioning, which is accessible to scientific investigation, but *all* I am is not contained or able to be described by the conceptualisations of the scientists. My actual existing is not intelligible to the concepts of science. The conceptualisations of science must be supplemented with other conceptualisations. An understanding of existing must be grounded in some other reality.

Anxious to avoid a return to a problematic dualism Shalom has to find a way of relating this 'I', this permanent existing, to physical processes:

I have to suppose that I am a subject who has somehow emerged in the course of specific physical processes, so that when I use words like *existing* and *permanence* I am necessarily talking *about* a physical process of which I am myself an integral part. And since I have rejected the theory that the 'I' as subject can be directly derived from physical and chemical processes per se, I must assume that what I mean by 'physical processes' or 'physical reality' is not identical with what the scientist means by 'physical processes' or 'physical reality', though what I mean obviously cannot contradict what the scientist means. (Shalom 1985, p. 426; original emphases)

Instead of absorbing the 'I' into 'mind' and 'body', Shalom absorbs the latter two into the 'I' which must therefore have its ground elsewhere. He remains nevertheless thoroughly committed to the physicalness of our 'I-ness'. Put in another way we can say that physical processes, in the widest sense, are carriers of our subjectivity:

the laws of physics are 'laws of physics and chemistry' by virtue of a more fundamental but inherent principle which determines them *to be* 'the laws of physics and chemistry'. Laws of this sort are shorthand expressions of concrete realities which they are unlikely to capture in their full existential complexity. But it is precisely in that existential complexity that physical processes can be per se the carriers of a subjectivity which will simply escape the generalisations that are the laws of science. In other words, subjectivity can in fact *be* a mode of organisation of those very physicochemical processes, of which the physicist and chemist know some of the 'laws', *without* that potential subjectivity having to appear in those 'laws'. (Shalom 1985, p. 434; original emphases)

We can all vouch for the 'reality' of our subjective experience. We do experience ourselves as having mind and body, and self-awareness, and consciousness, and something that many would concede can be described as spirit (even if we cannot agree on what it means). How does all this relate to the 'I'? Can we make sense of the categories of mind and body (at least) as a function of 'I-ness'?

In our experience of our reality we repeatedly observe physical and other processes. In the process of this observing we note regularities or patterns. We hold onto these observed regularities by naming them, and in so doing we make them into entities. In physics we call one regularity an atom, or another a black hole. In medicine we call a regular pattern a disease. Unfortunately we commonly go further and reify this disease pattern, and it becomes an entity which has too much finality. We assume we have it in our grasp; that now we know. The history of Newton and Einstein, as a major example outside medicine, shows how naive such assumptions can be. We believe that if we call something *clinical* depression, or obsessive-compulsive disorder, and particularly if we can describe some neurotransmitter abnormalities in the brain, then we have a substantial hold upon it, and we make it into a substantial reality. From our current observer position these patterns are the patterns we see, and we get useful mileage out of inferring laws from these patterns. Laws are abstracted generalisations derived from our limited observations of patterns. It is dangerous to assume too much finality from the patterns we observe, or to allow ourselves to be too restricted by the laws we have derived from the patterns (Shalom 1985).

What relevance does this have to our experience as 'I's who know we have minds and bodies (Shalom 1985)? Mind and body categories are themselves categories or regularities in our experience (our experience as 'I's) which we both perceive and name. They are important and dominant regularities in our subjective experience of ourselves as wholes. But they do not describe all of the whole. They must not be reified to entities which are then seen (when added together) as the best description of personhood. The perennial failure to resolve the mind/body problem by situating personhood as a composite of a dualistic pairing of mind and body is testimony to the failure of such reification.

There is also the matter of what we intuitively know. When I talk in seminars about the 'I' as fundamental it seems that many people from very different backgrounds lean forward and say 'Yes, yes, that's right'. We should assume that that which is fundamentally correct will have an intuitive feeling of congruence with reality. This seems to hold true in clinical practice. I find that when I talk to patients about mind/body issues, in a way which gets past their fears and acculturation, there is an inner hunger for seeing mind and body as one. Shalom makes the same point in respect of radical materialism, arguing that if the radical materialists were right in postulating matter as the ultimate fundamental (that is, reifying matter and giving it priority over all other aspects of personhood) then it would be easy for us all to accept this because at a deep level we would know this was in actual fact the real state of things:

the radical materialist [is in] something like an internally contra-dictory position. For he is holding the thesis that though, as sub-jectivities, we *should* be identifiable with purely material proc-esses, yet in terms of actual experiencing, we are *not* identifiable in that manner: we, in fact, have to involve a *theory* in order to convince ourselves that we are to be identified in that manner. And it seems to me that this is quite an untenable position to hold for a subjectivity which is supposed *to be* a purely material process. (Shalom 1985, p. 439; original emphases)

Where we have got to so far is to the position that the unity of the person is rooted in a reality of personal identity – which involves 'I', a subject, a permanence, an existing – of which the experience and expressions of mind and body are derivatives. But if we discard the dualistic mind/body conceptual framework for this more fundamental personal identity, how can we understand 'mind ... as a real potentiality written into certain kinds of physical bodies?' (Shalom 1985, p. 441).

Shalom calls on 'internalisation' to help us understand our aware-ness of mind and body as separate. This is a term which psychothera-pists understand very well, as a process which we use throughout life to develop our mental world. Schafer defines it in a way which would be acceptable to most psychotherapists: 'Internalisation refers to all those processes by which the subject transforms real or imaginary regulatory interactions with his environment, and real or imaginary characteristics of his environment, into inner regulations and charac-teristics' (Schafer 1968, p. 9). Shalom puts it a little more philosophi-cally when he remarks that internalisation is a potentiality, a capac-ity of the physical organism to 'discern the scope of what exists'.

Keeping Schafer's definition of internalisation in mind we can now summarise some of Shalom's postulates. First, there is no mind substance or separate mind. But living physical organisms do have a potential for subjectivity. A simple example may help. My eyes allow me to see red (just as an animal might see red). There is something else besides. I can also say to myself: 'I am seeing red.' I am self-aware. He is saying that humans (and, to a varying extent, other living organisms) have a potentiality for subjectivity, a potentiality which is inherent in physical processes. This subjectiv-ity is actualised by means of processes such as internalisation. As an infant I experience my own physicalness when I fall over and get hurt. This (and many other physical events) is repeated many times and in varying circumstances. The physical pain, the sight of the blood, and so on – the whole experience – becomes internalised, and I end up able to say not only that 'I have a body', but also that 'I have pain', or that 'I have a body in pain'. There is still more. I can actually reflect upon the fact that I can think about myself as a body in pain. It appears then that I have gone on to internalise my experience of my subjectivity. In this way then I observe the many and varied processes of my internalisations, and I see a repetition of such processes, and I can therefore say: 'I *have* a mind.' I have reified this recurrent experience, called it mind, and it becomes an entity. So certain sets of internalisations lead to the experience of *having* a body and a mind. The apparent mind/ body split is therefore based on internalised structuralisation of our experience.

I stated earlier that the pot cannot hold the potter in its hand. We can look outward (so to speak) from ourselves, from our 'I-ness', to the physical expression of our personhood (and of course to other physical realities), and describe it, but we are always looking outwards from the integrated source of our existence. We try and explain that source by encompassing it within the dimensions we see as we look out (our physicality, our mind, or combinations of the two) but it never works because they are derivatives of the whole rather than, when put together, a full description of the source.

There is a requirement therefore to be tentative, aware of the fact that there are limits, and the need for humility. Nevertheless, more can be said. There is the fascinating question of the so-called poles of permanence and change, which have already been alluded to. These concepts very much illuminate the notion of the 'I'. Shalom helps us understand permanence and change by considering the newly conceived human embryo.

A new conceptus is an identity from the beginning. The conceptus is a self-realising subject involving processes of change and continuity which can be seen clearly in the dimensions of both body and mind. Or, as Shalom puts it, the 'locus of subjectivity subtends both body and mind'. The crucial elements are beginning to emerge. The human subject from the beginning is characterised by *both* continuity and change – the pole of permanence and the pole of change; the former reflecting the previously postulated notion of the 'I' as a permanent existing. The constant and rapid changes in the conceptus' subjectivity, as it develops, are 'built on the permanence of that subjective locus of internalisation and actualisation'.

The pole of change describes the constant and rapid changes in the body and mind of the infant, and the reality of growth and development over linear time. Internalisation plays a huge role in this actualisation. In the process the infant realises (internalises) his or her subjectivity and is able, eventually, to say in a self-conscious way: 'I have a body', and, 'I have a mind'.

But the term 'pole of permanence' describes our 'I-ness' and personal identity, our continuity, our sense of timelessness; and it is this pole, or this locus, which gives me my 'me-ness'. In Shalom's words: 'identity ... is the conception of a permanent locus of all experience, a locus which gives structure, form, and content to a succession of changes which characterise *that* subject and no other' (Shalom 1985, pp. 450–2; original emphasis).

In our dualistic and scientistic way we tend to see physical processes as fundamentally inanimate. If we follow Shalom, it might seem that we must postulate some sort of vitalism which allows for a penetration of inanimate matter by some sort of new substance. Shalom asserts: 'there is nothing lurking *beneath* these chemical processes: there is something *involved* in these chemical processes, something that necessarily escapes the chemist because it is not a matter of chemistry' (1985, p.456; original emphases).

When he says that nothing lurks beneath the chemical processes, I do not think he is precluding unseen complexity. Rather, he is emphasising that he is not allowing another reality dualistically separate from the physical processes, and hidden behind them. The unseen reality is unseen merely because scientific techniques, and probes of physical reality, are not capable of discerning the reality of the subjective 'I'. He is saying that life is more than that which is described by science, and that 'more than' element certainly includes a capacity for subjectivity, reaching its summit in the 'I-ness' of the human.

The issue of permanence needs expansion. The events or processes which seem to be best encompassed at the pole of *change* clearly fit in with conventional linear time. An infant weighs 7 lb at birth and 15 lb weeks later. He talks at thirteen months. A girl menstruates at twelve, and a boy suddenly grows at fifteen. I retire at sixty-five and so on. It is all very linear, and comprehensible. But it appears that some of our functioning does not so easily fit this sort of time. Paul Davies' book *About Time* (1995) describes the current state of thinking in physics about concepts of time, thinking which certainly erodes confidence in our simplistic beliefs in a universal time, or just one sort of time existing everywhere. Day-to-day physical processes as seen by ordinary humans usually seem to fit within notions of linear time, but the things that cosmologists and physicists see with their new instruments cause them to struggle increasingly with linear and universal time concepts. But let us stay with the pole of permanence, the foetus, and personal identity.

The *physical* development of the foetus is rapid, involving aspects of mind and body encompassed by the *pole of change*, and the changes are easily accommodated within notions of linear time. But Shalom argues that *identity* with its *pole of permanence* must involve a different sort of time. This is fascinating because it comes close to Bohm's work (see p. 159). It is also fascinating because of its affinity with Freud's notion that the unconscious was characterised by timelessness.

What Shalom is saying is that personal identity has something to do with nontemporality (or quasi-nontemporality), or is independent of linear time as we know it, whilst the processes usually observed by scientific methods have to do with linear time. This nontemporal aspect, my 'I-ness', gives rise to the aspects of myself characterised by the pole of change: 'What this situation would mean for the chemical processes involved is that they are the processes that they are *because* of the particular kind of subtending quasi-nontemporality *of* that particular kind of subjectivity' (Shalom 1985, p. 456; original emphases). He is saying here that the unique character of the 'I' gives rise to, or subtends, the unique manifestations at the pole of change, in the body and mind (as they are called once they are reified). Each living and conscious entity becomes by ennumerable internalisations the actualised entity expressive of its potential subjectivity (p. 460).

All of this helps us to understand why we easily make the mind/body distinction. The human deploys two processes of internalisation: 'the internalisation of physical processes *in* the locus of permanence, and the internalisation *of* the locus of permanence itself, together with all its internalised physical processes, *to* itself' (Shalom 1985, p. 462; original emphases). Put very simply, this seems to mean that my awareness of myself as *body* is a consequence of internalisation, to the pole of permanence, of my physical experience of myself. My awareness of myself as *mind* is a consequence of internalisation of the experience of myself as a pole of permanence.

All living organisms are seen by Shalom as having some potential for subjectivity, and this potential comes in higher and higher forms. He acknowledges the mystery and obscurity of life, holding nevertheless to the view that we are better off with the mystery of personal identity than we are in trying to unite mind and body out of a dualistic materialism:

The postulation of a potential subjectivity – founded on quasi-

nontemporality – avoids the impossible problem of understanding how *chemistry as such* can become an instinct ... we situate
these processes where they belong: in the obscurity of the tem-
poral existing of the physical organisms which develop, *by their
means*, into the specific animals that surround us, and of which
we ourselves are exemplifications. (Shalom 1985, p. 457; original emphases)

An increasing capacity for internalisation allows for a finer and
finer appreciation of the world and its physical processes. But it is
the internalisation of the pole of permanence to itself which is the
crucial issue for self-awareness:

what this ... implies ... is that the existential mystery of a potential subjectivity, the existential mystery of the quasi-temporality of
the permanence polarity ... becomes partially intelligible by revealing itself to itself as that which becomes a 'self-conscious subject',
an 'I', a human person ... it is an existential locus which not only
internalises the processes of physical reality, but that is also itself
internalisable, giving rise to its own self-realisation *as* a locus of
quasi-nontemporality. We call the results of this further operation
'self-awareness'. (Shalom 1985, p. 460; original emphases)

Where we have got to is the notion of personhood which
involves the priority of personal identity, the 'I' as existing, over
any notions of mind, body or spirit. These latter terms are valid in
the sense that they are concepts which describe our experience as
'I's. Put together in one way or another, in hierarchies, or in
combinations, they never solve the problem of integration. But seen
as understandable derivatives of our experience as 'I's which have
self-awareness, we find that much of the struggle around mind/
body problems can drop away. The 'I' will actualise over linear
time. Therefore physical and psychological development will have a
sense of both continuity and change, and will seem to be underpinned by a permanence which is an essential characteristic of the
'I'. In matters of disease and illness we should expect both physical
elements and 'story', as nondualistic manifestations of the same 'I',
in different dimensions. Nothing in all this excludes the possibility
of complex derivative processes which would allow us to construe
illnesses in terms of somatopsychosomatic sequences, or the like.
That does not imply a fundamental dualism, but a layering of
complexity beyond the fundamental holism implied by seeing the
person best described as a personal identity, or as an 'I'.

The work of Shalom provides a philosophical basis for a true nondualistic holism, which will be attractive to some but not all. Whilst embracing physicality he declines a physico-materialist fundamentalism. Stated in very simple terms, he argues for a more fundamental personal identity which is expressed in the physical, and yet is *not* fully described by the physical. He is not a vitalist for whom the body is some sort of garment clothing the more genuine reality. The body is a vital dimension of the person. Matter is seen as including, in living organisms, a potential for subjectivity (seen in its ultimate form in human beings as the experience of 'I-ness'); a potential not seen by scientific instruments because they only operate in the restricted dimension of physical experience.

The obvious question is, can one go any further than this? What is the origin of this personal identity? Just as things are starting to get interesting, does one leap from this to articles of religious faith? For some this may be a natural corollary, but there are other nonreligious explorations, not primarily from the philosophical arena, which tend to support the drift of Shalom's philosophical work.

The New Physics and Holism

The ideas of the theoretical physicist David Bohm have been embraced by some as providing a theoretical underpinning for New Age practices of one sort or another. *The Holographic Paradigm and Other Paradoxes* (Wilber 1985) provides a useful resource for reading Bohm (and other New Age theorists) discussing the nature of reality. I want to use Bohm's work to shake up our presuppositions in such a way that it becomes more conceivable that we do not have to stop at a vague but essential theory of personal identity. My first introduction to Bohm was in Peters' *The Cosmic Self* (1991), which is really a critique of the New Age movement from a Christian perspective. But its main attraction for me is the chapter on 'The New Physics and the Holistic Cosmology' which provides a lucid summary of Bohm's thought and new ideas bearing on holism. Peters calls Bohm 'the scientific mascot of new age consciousness'. He is a scientist who proffers a scientific language or paradigm for the unification, synthesis and integration of the fragmented world, both within and without.

Modern thinking is characterised by atomism, mechanism, objectivism and physicalism, and this is seen by many as a legacy of the work of Newton and Descartes. In Peters' view the Newtonian paradigm is characterised by:

- 3-dimensional space

- Time flowing from past to future

- A time/space 'receptacle' (which contains nature's law and the course of events)

- A fundamental materiality

- Matter is viewed as passive and inert

- Relationships between the elements of matter are determined by external forces (for example, gravity)

- A closed causal nexus is assumed

- Definite causes give rise to definite effects – there is an implicit and rigorous mechanical determinism

- If we know enough the future can be predicted (Peters 1991, pp. 136–7)

This list dramatically emphasises the world view which dominates Western thinking. If we were to think about our personal experience of doctors, many of us would recognise that generally doctors think about our illnesses in a way which is almost entirely circumscribed by the Newtonian model.

The same is true in respect to Descartes. Peters states very aptly that 'the net effect' of Descartes' emphasis on 'the world of extended objects out there and the world of subjectivity in our own mind ... has been to cause us to attempt to separate human consciousness from the world processes and, in addition, by concentrating on the plurality of objects, to miss seeing the world process as a single whole' (1991, p. 137).

I suspect most of us trained in medicine would recognise our own rootedness in these Newtonian and Cartesian presuppositions. But these presuppositions are being disturbed by new developments in physics. Peters summarises Einstein's special theory of relativity as having 'dispossessed the framework of absolute space and time ... Thus, the idea of a uniform receptacle of space and time had to be surrendered at least in certain domains of physical research' (1991, p. 137).

Then there is quantum theory and experimentation which:

sees atomic particles [travelling] from one location to another without traversing the distance in between ... it is helpful ... to understand them also as waves. ...

recognises that no apparent structure of efficient causation belongs to individual subatomic events. ...

demonstrates nonlocal relationships between electrons – when two electrons from a single atom have interacted and then flown off in opposite directions, interference with one will instantly affect the other, regardless of the distance between them ... This is action at a distance, action with no connection. What we have here, astonishingly, is a noncausal, nonmaterial, yet influential relationship. In short, quantum theory takes us away from a material notion of matter and a closed nexus of efficient causation, away from a strictly mechanistic picture of the world. (Peters 1991, pp. 137–8)

If we accept these relatively new findings as having relevance in a general way to all of reality then we have to start to question our fundamental presuppositions. At a macroscopic and microscopic level the Newtonian view works pretty well, but at a subatomic level it comes into serious question. Are we practising our medicine within a circumscribed compartment with inherently limited possibilities of resolution of disease because the origins and processes of disease are not limited to this compartment or view of reality?

The scene is now set for Bohm's new paradigm. We have allowed ourselves to think in compartmentalisations, and the apparent divisions in the world (for example, mind and body) are really artefacts of our compartmentalising world view. They may also be the result of a natural tendency within us to make sense of the world. We tend to separate things into categories so as to comprehend, and make some order within the enormous complexity. In a way categorisation is a reflection of our finiteness: we have a limited capacity to comprehend the whole. This is exactly what Shalom is saying. Bohm puts this in different terms and asserts that, as scientists (and physicians), we are preoccupied by the explicate order in the world. The explicate order consists of the macroscopic and microscopic aspects of reality. The new physics suggests that beneath this, or perhaps interior to it, is an implicate order characterised by Bohm as 'undivided wholeness in flowing movement'. For our purposes Peters' summary of this idea is helpful:

Flow means that everything is changing. But it is not a single homogeneous or undifferentiated flow, which would be undiscernible from static being. It is rather a flux, a movement of forms, shapes, and units. Despite the undivided wholeness in the overall flowing movement, we can by tools of thought abstract from it patterns, objects, entities, conditions, structures, and so on, and these have a certain autonomy and stability. What Bohm wants to stress here is that the flow as an unknown and undefinable totality is prior, whereas the flux of describable events and objects is considered an abstraction. This means that our knowledge of the laws of physics deals with abstractions; it deals with events and objects having only relative independence and existence from their ultimate ground in the unknown totality of the universal movement. (1991, p. 143)

So, from the point of view of the physician, the stable and autonomous patterns, structures, entities, and so on, in the explicate order, are such things as persons, body organs and physiological processes. The processes of perception and thinking (as well as the instruments we have created to extend these faculties, such as microscopes and laboratory tests) cause us to see and experience reality at this level. This is a level of reality which we easily recognise because of the way we are constructed, and which we easily restrict ourselves to because of the various reasons postulated throughout this book. But these explicate realities are nevertheless abstractions of the more fundamental implicate reality, just as diagnostic categories of disease are taxonomic abstractions, created by the observing clinician. These latter seem so cohesively sensible. It seems so obvious to declare asthma to be asthma on the basis that the patient wheezes and the airway is hyper-reactive. This is very much a description of asthma confined to the explicate order. But we might eventually find that asthma could be more fundamentally described in terms of anger, or interpersonal separation/individuation, or, I suppose, in Bohmian terms, as some characteristic disturbance within the holomovement, or as some sort of spiritual perturbation (or perhaps in terms of all of these).

It becomes more complicated than this, however. There are new concepts of mind emerging as well, and these have implications of great relevance to the mind/body-oriented clinician. According to Peters:

It follows that human knowing is both an abstraction from and a participation in the total flux. It is an abstraction because when we focus on either subjective knowing or objective knowledge, we temporarily forget the wider unity that binds them. We mentally extricate them from the single flow of which they are a part. And although the distinction between mind and matter is described by Bohm as an abstraction from a prior unity in the universal flux, such things as mind and matter do exist. But they do not exist by themselves, independently, in isolation. They are each modes of the one common underlying reality. 'Mind and matter are not separate substances. Rather, they are different aspects of one whole and unbroken movement'. (1991, p. 143)

Again this sounds in many ways like Shalom, but Bohm's focus is not so much the 'I' but the reality which lies beneath the explicate order of individuals, objects and the ordinarily manifest world. Originally I was startled by this material coming as I was out of a dualistic framework. I found myself resonating with it as well, because although trained in macroscopic clinical aspects of mind and body, I had come to recognise that patients presented with somatic and mental phenomena which seemed to be representations, in two different dimensions, of a common unitary reality. Now from a totally different and sub-microscopic vantage point some physicists were saying something that at least sounded similar; that mind and body were different abstractions of a common underlying reality. Later I was to discover Shalom saying the same thing from a philosophical perspective.

Although my intention here is to let these concepts provoke the reader's thinking rather than attempt to create a definitive clinically useful hypothesis I will try now to summarise some more specific details of Bohm's model and some of its implications.

It appears then, in Bohm's model, that we can no longer separate thought and so-called real objects. The underlying flow or holomovement is thoughtful, it has consciousness. This clearly has some superficial affinity with Shalom's conclusion that matter has an inherent potentiality for subjectivity.

In addition there is an 'implicate order' by which it is meant that the whole is in some way represented in the abstracted parts. These parts are called 'subtotalities'. The nonmanifest implicate order is primary and is expressed in explicate manifestations perceptible to human senses. As Peters says: 'the manifest world consists in the external unfolding or explication of the implicate order', but we are under illusion 'when we assume that what is explicate is all there is' (1991, p. 145). The unfolded explicate manifestations have much variety, with varying degrees of intelligence and consciousness, or, perhaps in Shalom's terms, subjectivity.

I hope the reader can get a 'feel' for these rather foreign propositions. Put very simply, we might say that humans are entities with form and structure expressed in the dimensions we call mind and the body, each of which is representative of the living flow which is seen as the underlying reality. Whether the flow or holomovement is the final underlying reality is of course another question. It could be a named abstraction created by our increasing ability to perceive subatomic reality!

But in all this there is something missing. We seem to be turning away from the fragmented atomism or fundamental pluralism of the materialist view to a holism 'that swallows up everything individual into mystical absorption' (Peters 1991, p. 148). Within my practice of integrative medicine I have discovered my own tendencies to reductionism. Once one sees the power of the mind/body approach it is very tempting to approach everything in that way, just as the biomaterialists have seen all reality within the Newtonian paradigm. But actually in the Bohmian view there is room for the pluralism and categories we see in the explicate order. He specifies categories called 'subtotalities' or what Arthur Koestler calls 'holons':

> There are no completely distinguishable parts and wholes in any absolute sense. They mutually define and depend on one another. Furthermore, all things are held together by an intermediate reality, the subwhole or holon. The holon is a stable, integrated structure, equipped with self-regulatory devices and enjoying a considerable degree of autonomy, of self-government. (Peters 1991, p. 148)

Interpreting this, one could perhaps say that a human being is an example of a holon or subtotality, and indeed an organ of the body (heart, kidney, lung) would be a subtotality at a lower level.

There are so many questions to be asked. How autonomous is the individual, really, and what are the 'connections' between individuals? Some astonishing possibilities jump to mind. When a child appears to have an illness as an expression of her mother's psychopathology, how is this projected onto the child? Is this purely through subtle psychological 'influence' (and what does that now mean?) or are there other forms of connectedness? If a human is a holon, manifesting at explicate level in the abstractions we call mind and body, what is the underlying primary implicate reality? Is it enough just to call it holomovement or flow?

According to Bohm:

the more comprehensive, deeper, and more inward actuality is neither mind nor body but rather a yet higher-dimensional actuality, which is their common ground and which is of a nature beyond both ... In this higher-dimensional ground the implicate order prevails. Thus, within this ground, *what is* is movement which is represented in thought as the co-presence of many phases of the implicate order ... So we do not say that mind and body causally affect each other, but rather that the movements of both are the outcome of related projections of a common higher-dimensional ground. (Bohm 1980, p. 209)

Shalom takes us from mind and body to the 'I' that exists. Following Bohm, this individual 'I' is some sort of holonic manifestation in the explicate order, rooted in an implicate order, a higher-dimensional ground. For Bohm the consciousness of the individual 'I' appears to be some sort of projection from the holomovement into an individual form. Many new questions arise which are beyond the scope of this volume. Is the holomovement the final ground, or the best way of describing fundamental reality? I very much doubt it. But Shalom and Bohm serve us well by modelling exploration of new ways of seeing reality which honour our intuitive awareness of our wholeness, which honour modern thought and scientific experiment, which challenge the narrow parameters of dualistic physico-materialism and, most importantly, allow practitioners like myself to create models of personhood which are holistic, and which imply models of healing which are potentially much more efficacious than a model based around a 'machine' paradigm of personhood.

Those of us who are spiritually inclined may be tempted to speculate in a variety of ways about the relationship of all this to spirituality. Thus the holomovement becomes the divine life force for the New Age adherent; in essence, a new monism. Christians, on the other hand, may want to modify the ideas to retain notions of a God who expresses himself in all things (including the holomovement), sustaining all things; a God who is both immanent *and* other, and would thus perhaps look for greater reality beyond the holomovement.

Whatever our preferences and speculations, Bohm's ideas profoundly challenge our grossly simplistic materialistic assumptions, and I hope that the reader will not so much accept the propositions as start to question his or her own assumptions and, in doing so, perhaps start to look at patients and their illnesses in a different way. For me, the ideas expressed here have assisted me in breaking out of the constraints of dualistic, linear, materialistic and deterministic thinking. I am attracted by the potential of these ideas for integration of body/mind/spirit but it would be naive to assume them as truth, let alone final truth. But they do invite an intellectual elasticity, and for me new dimensions of creativity, as I ponder new models of understanding human disease.

Earlier in this chapter I raised the possibility that disease could be described as some sort of 'core disturbance' which may be expressed in *both* mind and body. In Shalom's terms this might be some sort of aberration in the 'I' which subtends mind and body. Bohm might see a core disturbance as an aberration or perturbation at either holonic or the holomovement levels. What such aberrations might be are only speculative, but certainly the world's religions would have notions which might be contributory. One might consider developmental theories in this light and wonder if relational problems (between mother and foetus, or infant) could be framed in terms of the holomovement and its disturbed expression (whatever that might be) within and between individuals. New Age thinkers tend to conceptualise in these terms.

There are of course more traditional religious views of a putative core disturbance. For Western Christian tradition the core disturbance has been rooted in some sort of personal alienation from God. This view seems to be rooted in a notion that the spiritual pervades our whole personhood, and its 'energy' and presence is represented in both our somatic and psychological realities. This way of talking about the spiritual may be too compartmentalising, and it leads away from the holistic to the spiritual. We are unitary beings with somatic, psychological and spiritual aspects. Although some might consider the spiritual aspect as fundamental (an idealist position), I favour the view that the term 'spiritual' does not so much denote another (primary) compartment, but rather is a way of emphasising the reality of our lively holistic connectedness with the transcendent. Bohm's theories might be interpreted as supporting this, from a modern physics perspective.

Second, traditional Christianity would argue that the core disturbance has something to do with a disturbance of this lively connectedness with the transcendent. This is a view that suggests that disease has something to do with an individual's relationship (or perhaps dysrelationship) with the transcendent. One might see this as having some similarities or parallels with the theories of disease based on the primary importance of early developmental relational problems, or of some disturbance of the holomovement. Perhaps these concepts should not be seen as alternative theories but as different selections of data from complex multilayered reality, taken from different vantage points.

This brief review of some of the possibilities in relation to a primary 'core disturbance' could be greatly amplified, but this is a task for another volume.

10 INDIVIDUALS VERSUS GROUPS

Those researchers who have allied themselves with collaborators from disciplines other than their own – whatever these may be – are especially aware of and, perhaps, the most likely to tolerate the ambiguity and the complexity that necessarily arise if one is sensitive to the interdependence of systems. At the same time, an appreciation of the integrated nature of adaptive functions unveils breathtaking glimpses of panoramas that are not even hinted at by any single component of the scene. Psychoneuroimmunology, if not the most conspicuous, is the most recent example of a scientific field that has developed and now prospers by exploring and tilling fertile territories secreted by the arbitrary and illusory boundaries of the biomedical sciences. Disciplinary boundaries, codified by bureaucracies, are historical fictions that can restrict the imagination and the technologies that can lend credence to Werner Heisenberg's assertion that *'What we observe is not nature itself, but nature exposed to our method of questioning'.* (Ader, 1995, p. ix; emphasis added)

Even the most casual of photographers knows the frustration of trying to capture the impact of an awesome sweeping landscape around him by taking the best possible shot, and yet being left feeling that the photograph hardly does justice to the original experience. Showing the picture to a friend, he says rather lamely: 'You should have been there.' The technology is superb, the photograph is beautiful, but the boundaries imposed by the method necessarily limit that which can be seen and experienced.

The Primacy Given to Measurement

Mainstream somatic medicine – internal medicine, surgery, pathology – is dominated by an implicit, and at times explicit, biological reductionism, and recently Rotov (1991) has argued that the same is also true of psychological medicine, or psychiatry. This skew towards biological reductionism is in part related to the way doctors and scientists are trained to observe things. This is a crucial matter. This book is based on what has been learned from meeting and working with patients and clients, as individuals seen in depth. The 'technology' is listening – to the individual's story, or listening to an individual who is story-telling. The technique is listening and the focus is the individual's story, and that is what is captured in the process. With the passage of time, of course, an individual becomes part of a *group* of individuals who have been worked with. That may seem a rather unnecessary statement, but the process in which an individual becomes seen as a member of a group creates problems for some of the individual data, especially if the observer focus comes off the individual and on to the group.

The individual approach invites the scorn of those who shun anecdote, and there are indeed many problems with method based solely in anecdote. Rotov's points on this issue have great relevance to holism, and to the approach enjoined here. His comments were offered in the context of a trenchant criticism of the American 1988 National Plan for Schizophrenia Research, which he sees as preoccupied with the study of groups, resulting in a neglect of the individual.

First, Rotov questions the modern scientific primacy given to statistical studies of groups of individuals. This is heresy to a modern clinician. He says that this scientific insistence on measurement as the final arbiter of reality is: 'the key characteristic of physicalism, a reductionistic doctrine that teaches that all mental phenomena can be explained in terms of the laws of physics' (Rotov 1991, p. 184). The clinician's method of observation is both dominated by and restricted by measurement. The patient's *story*, for example, which cannot be measured, is ignored.

Rotov deplores another by-product of the measurement and statistical approach, which he calls the practice of 'essentialisation'. By this he means that when we focus on data gleaned from statistical studies of groups we end up with the truth that derives from what individuals have in common, but we lose the truth which is highly individual. What has happened is that the method selects, compares and analyses patient data categories common to the group. Using Ader's words, and Heisenberg's emphasis, from the quote opening this chapter, it could be said that 'an arbitrary and illusory boundary' has been created between the group data and the individual data by the methods used by the clinician to observe nature.

For example, let us take a group of patients with urticaria caused by somatisation. Essentialisation leads to a focus on what these patients have in common. This is what diagnosis is essentially – a regular pattern with a name. In this particular disorder called urticaria, essentialisation, or the group focus, leads us to certain typical common elements such as lesions on the skin, or mast cell degranulation, or a clinical response to antihistamines. But an individual focus on the patient, in depth, allows us to see that one person has urticaria as a manifestation of a failed grief reaction, and another is unconsciously angry with her husband. These nuances are totally missed unless one spends focused time with each patient as an individual. The importance of this is that healing for the individual patient comes when these individual issues are resolved.

Measurement is of great value but if given primacy the clinician becomes somatically preoccupied and nonholistic, and the patient is left with a restricted and impoverished physicalist medical response. Generally speaking, this is the state of modern medicine and psychiatry. Rotov (1991) points out that the 'laboratory idols' of physicalism, methodology, jargon, objectivity, mathematisation, measurement, standardisation, instruments and rating scales do not allow much room for crucial human characteristics such as willing, feeling and intentionality, let alone fundamental psychotherapeutic matters such as intrapsychic conflict. Anyone with psychotherapy experience of mind/body disorders will recognise that it is the latter group of qualities which have to be grappled with in any therapeutic resolution of the problems underlying the disorders. Suzanne Langer, the American philosopher, called these qualities 'the embarrassing elements – [such as] willing, intending, feeling – that is, all words for introspectively known factors' (1967). It is the thesis of this book that these embarrassing elements, the phenomenology of our conscious and unconscious experience, actually matter to, and are an unseen dimension in, the development of many illnesses.

Pataki wrote recently that: 'Love, friendship, caring for oneself and for others, loss of others and the loss of one's self in madness or death concern us more in daily life, art, literature (though they do not much concern contemporary psychiatry and Anglo-Saxon philosophy) than anything else' (1996, p. 57). Nor do such things concern modern medicine in its understanding of pathology. But love and friendship, and a host of other such qualities, are at the centre of the concerns of this book.

It is not being argued that measurement should be abandoned. The problem is not measurement, but the preoccupation with that which can be measured. Rotov (1991) says rather strongly that preoccupation with measurement leads to a 'shallow materialism'.

Eschewing measurement is likely to lead to equally inadequate or erroneous descriptions of reality. This is seen in some forms of alternative medicine or the New Age movement, both of which are starting to have real impact on the practice of medicine, but are hardly constrained at all by the disciplines of measurement. One problem is of course that measurement is difficult in the mind/body area. There may be ultimate realities which cannot ever be measured. Measurement may be applicable to certain states of reality but not to others. Be this as it may, it can be confidently stated that measurement based on limited (physicalist) presuppositions, and the essentialising approach, is going to yield limited results. Measurement based in erroneous presuppositions is going to yield erroneous results. Measurement should continue but there must be a focus on the individual and his or her individual story to allow discovery of data from which new presuppositions, and perhaps new ways of measuring, can be developed.

Put very simply, the argument is that we must move away from treating patients merely as biochemical machines and objects of measurement. We must embrace the whole, and attend to the psychospiritual dimensions of personal experience, and begin to see how crucial these are. We see what we look at, and just because we can get a *handle* on the physical by measurement, there is no justification for ignoring other aspects of the person.

The Language of the Body

The holistic task is very difficult. Reducing the person to that which is currently measurable is untenable, but is it really possible to get very far by in-depth study of an individual with whom the clinician is in relationship? Joyce McDougall, a psychoanalyst, provides a stimulating contribution to this question in her book *Theatres of the Body* (1989), in which she discusses the psychotherapy of physical illnesses. A major emphasis is on the concept of disease or illness as language. For most clinicians such a concept is preposterous, but in working with somatisers over the years I have gradually come to see that in a patient's *choice* of disorder it is often possible to discern a statement, or a language of the body. Illness (or some illnesses) seen from this perspective is construed as a form of communication.

A sixty-year-old woman came with a florid facial rash, of five years' standing, resistant to all previous treatments. She had even had her liver biopsied on suspicion of a carcinoid tumour. She was referred for an allergy opinion but I could find no evidence of allergic factors. But in response to my question, 'What has been the most difficult thing in your life over the last six years?', she promptly replied: 'My husband's illness.' I then asked her how it had affected her, and she said: 'Oh, I keep a brave face on it.' Noting her choice of words I asked her the same question five minutes later, and again she used the same wording. I drew her attention to the possible linkage between her facial rash and the 'brave face'. A week later I spent a further hour providing a cathartic opportunity for her bottled up feelings, and within ten days from first assessment her rash had gone.

This rash appears to have been a statement, in the soma, of things unable to be expressed in verbal language. It is a moot point whether her healing was due to putting the feelings in verbal language, or whether it was due to the fact that at last she was heard. The former implies that the issue is a failure on her part to put psychological matters into their proper medium of language, that is, illness occurring because of poor handling of feelings. The latter implies that the issue is a question of whether anybody listening to her heard what she had to say, that is, illness as a manifestation of the inadequacy of relationship. These issues have been discussed in Chapter 9. Whatever the case, this lady's rash was an excellent example of a somatic metaphor. Though many people have facial rashes, this story is highly individual and probably unique; that is, it could be imagined that behind a grouping of facial rashes there will be as many unique stories as there are individuals.

McDougall (1989) furnishes many examples of disease as language. Much of her emphasis is on core affective states and conflicts generated in early infancy, when the child has no verbal language to act as a vehicle for intense emotion. The body becomes an obvious theatre for playing out these powerful dramas. Adults with alexithymia (seemingly having no language for feelings) are seen as being in a similar situation. This all leads to a view of physical disease not merely as some sort of biological disarray, but as a crystallisation of a complex set of interacting processes including the somatic and the psychological, and to do with language and relationship. In this view I find myself closely aligned with McDougall. My approach to the psychotherapy of somatic disorders is rather different to hers. We share an emphasis on object relations theory, self psychology, and interpersonal theory, but I am less Freudian and often work in a briefer psychotherapeutic mode.

It is not of course possible to see language in every disease process. This is partly because to reduce everything to language would be just another absurd reductionism. Language aspects of disease may be present but currently unintelligible. There are other complexities. For example, who is the patient addressing: him or herself, or a significant other? Does the body have a limited vocabulary? Is an irritable bowel simply a common expression of many types of story? Can organs or bodily systems be seen as conduit systems for emotional energies which are not being discharged in other more appropriate ways? In this way some diseases might be seen as having general but not specific communicative value. On the other hand, some disorders are powerfully, vividly and specifically communicative. Complexity rules.

The Taxonomic Response to Complexity

The traditional response to this complexity has been to develop taxonomic classifications of disease which largely reflect the essentialising group approach referred to above. These classifications are unable to give any insight into the individual 'story' elements. In effect they lead away from the individual to his or her disease projections. Nevertheless, there have been attempts to classify mind/body disorders in ways which hint at the heterogeneity of origin of these disorders, and the rich variety of clinical presentation.

For example, the complexity immediately apparent in Lipowski's classification of somatoform disorders underscores the naivety of any attempt to oversimplify in this area. His categories are as follows (my comments in italics):

1. Subjectively perceived physiological concomitants of affects which may be regarded as integral components (or equivalents) of the affect and are devoid of any primary symbolic meaning eg. blanching with anger. *This category implies that there are affects accompanied by simple physical concomitants with no primary symbolic meaning. Certainly some somatoform manifestations seem much simpler than others. Blanching is perhaps a normal and universal physical projection of the 'I' who is angry.*

2. Somatic changes symbolically expressing ideational content. *For example, the above lady with the facial rash, or a patient*

*with conversion disorder blindness. Here we have an increased
dimension of complexity. The physical manifestation 'tells' a
more elaborate story.*

3. Secondary symbolic elaborations of perceived bodily changes
regardless of their origin. *For example, facial aging 'lines' becoming the focus of underlying fears of dying. Here we have the
inner 'story' taking a 'ride' on some bodily characteristic to
provide both a focus and a justification for itself.*

4. Excessive preoccupation with bodily sensations and functions,
normal and abnormal (hypochondriacal syndromes).

5. Nosophobia ie. dread of disease or suffering.

6. Somatic delusions as seen in schizophrenia.

7. Communication of psychological distress in somatic metaphors. (Lipowski 1968, p. 394)

It should be noted that Lipowski does not acknowledge directly,
in this classification, the possibility that many common physical
diseases, generally accepted as being purely 'somatic', may have a
place amongst the categories, though I suspect that many of the
disorders described in this book, and many others presenting in all
types of medical practice, may actually fit very well into categories
2 and 7.

Classifications like this underscore the potential complexity to
be confronted in patients and clients with physical disorders,
when viewed from an integrative perspective. They also emphasise the point that as soon as we classify we immediately
constrict our field of view. Whilst we must classify, we must
ensure that the boundaries to our classifications are left open.
Currently much medical thinking, and most taxonomic systems,
actually exclude from clinical consideration those human subjective 'story' elements which we all regard as crucial to our lived
experience. We must include them despite the difficulties we
confront as we begin to do so. Much of the difficulty arises from
our Western philosophical heritage, some arises from our individual defensive reluctance to face inner reality both in our
patients and in ourselves, and some arises from the fact that if
we try and consider multiple aspects of reality, life tends to
become less manageable. Whatever the underlying reasons, there

is no doubt that most clinicians in medicine and psychotherapy are unaccustomed to thinking in the ways set forth in this book. I can conclude by testifying to one comforting reality – with practice it gets a lot easier.

References

Ader, R. (1995) Foreword, in B.E. Leonard and K. Miller (eds), *Stress, the Immune System and Psychiatry*. Chichester: John Wiley and Sons Ltd.

American Psychiatric Association (1994) *Diagnostic and Statistical Manual of Mental Disorders* IV. Washington DC.

Bain, S.T. and Spaulding, W.B. (1967) 'The Importance of Coding Presenting Symptoms', *Canadian Medical Association Journal* 97: 953–9.

Benson, H. (1995) 'Placebo Effect and Remembered Wellness', *Mind/Body Medicine* 1: 44–5.

Bohm, D. (1980) *Wholeness and the Implicate Order*. London: Routledge and Kegan Paul.

Bridges, K.W. and Goldberg, D.P. (1985) 'Somatic Presentation of DSM III Psychiatric Disorders in Primary Care', *Journal of Psychosomatic Research* 29: 563–9.

Broom, B.C. (1990) 'A Practical Approach to Psychosomatic Problems in Medical Non-Psychiatric Settings', *Journal of Christian Health Care* 3: 13–23.

Brown, T.M. (1988) 'Cartesian Dualism and Psychosomatics', *Psychosomatics* 30: 322–31.

Cabot, R. (1903) 'Truth and Falsehood in Medicine', *American Medicine* 5: 344.

Campbell, K. (1984) *Body and Mind*. Indiana: Notre Dame Press, 2nd edn.

Davies, P. (1995) *About Time*. Harmondsworth, Middlesex: Viking, Penguin Books Ltd.

Dulles, A. (1983) *Models of Revelation*. Dublin: Gill and Macmillan Ltd.

Goldberg, D.P. and Bridges, K. (1988) 'Somatic Presentations of

Psychiatric Illness in Primary Care Setting', *Journal of Psychosomatic Research* 32: 137–44.

Groddeck, G. (1977) *The Meaning of Illness*. London: Hogarth Press / Institute of Psychoanalysis.

Kleinman, A. and Kleinman, J. (1985) 'Somatisation: the Interconnections in Chinese Society among Culture, Depressive Experiences, and the Meanings of Pain', in A. Kleinman and B. Good (eds), *Culture and Depression*. University of California Press.

Langer, S.K. (1967) *Mind: An Essay on Human Feeling*. Baltimore, MD: The Johns Hopkins University Press.

Levenson, E.A. (1974) 'Changing Concepts of Intimacy in Psychoanalytic Practice', *Contemporary Psychoanalysis* 10: 359–69.

Lipowski, Z.J. (1968) 'Review of Consultation Psychiatry and Psychosomatic Medicine III: Theoretical Issues', *Psychosomatic Medicine* 30: 394–422.

Lipowski, Z.J. (1986) 'Somatisation: a Borderland between Medicine and Psychiatry', *Canadian Medical Association Journal* 135: 609–709.

McDougall, J. (1989) *Theatres of the Body*. London: Free Association Books.

Pam, A. (1995) Introduction, in C.A. Ross and A. Pam (eds), *Pseudoscience in Biological Psychiatry: Blaming the Body*. New York: J Wiley and Sons, Inc.

Pataki, T. (1996) 'Psychoanalysis, Psychiatry, and Philosophy', *Quadrant*, April.

Peters, T. (1991) *The Cosmic Self. A Penetrating Look at Today's New Age Movements*. San Francisco: Harper.

Pribram, K. (1985) 'What the Fuss is All About' in K. Wilber (ed.), *The Holographic Paradigm and Other Paradoxes*. Boston and London: Shambhala Publications Inc.

Ross, R.L., Hamilton, G.E. and Smith, R.G. (1995) 'Somatisation Disorder in Primary Care', *Mind/Body Medicine* 1: 24–9.

Rotov, M. (1991) 'Phenomenology or Physicalism?', *Schizophrenia Bulletin* 17: 183–6.

Schact, L. (1977) Introduction, G. Groddeck, *The Meaning of Illness*. London: Hogarth Press / Institute of Psychoanalysis.

Schafer, R. (1968) *Aspects of Internalisation*. New York: International Universities Press.

Shalom, A. (1985) *The Body/Mind Conceptual Framework and the Problem of Personal Identity*. Atlantic Highlands, N.J.: Humanities Press International, Inc.

Smith, R.C. (1985) 'A Clinical Approach to the Somatising Patient', *Journal of Family Practice* 21: 294–301.

Strupp, H.H. and Blackwood, G.L. (1980) 'Recent Methods of Psychotherapy', in H.I. Kaplan, A.M. Freedman and B.J. Sadock (eds), *Comprehensive Textbook of Psychiatry III*. Baltimore/London: Williams and Wilkins.

Weber, R. (1985) The Physicist and the Mystic – is a Dialogue between them possible? A Conversation with David Bohm, in K. Wilber (ed.), *The Holographic Paradigm and Other Paradoxes*. Boston and London: Shambhala Publications, Inc.

White, V. (1952) *God and the Unconscious: An Encounter Between Psychology and Religion*. Cleveland and New York: Meridian Books, 3rd edn, 1969.

Wilber, K. (1985) (ed.) *The Holographic Paradigm and Other Paradoxes*. Boston and London: Shambhala Publications, Inc.

Index